THIS
Is a Book

Not available as an e-book, i-book, Cybook, nook book, Bebook, Kindle book, pdf, opf, EPUB, Plucker, TealDoc, TomeRaider, HTML, TEI, XMDF, CSS, Compressed HM, RAR, TAR, ACE, ZIP, DAISY, DjVu, IEC 62448, XML, ICARUS, iLiad, eStick, Open eBook, Newton eBook, Nexus eBook, Broadband eBook, Multimedia eBook, FictionBook, PocketBook, Rocketbook, Flip Book, fake spam book, text floating in a "cloud" somewhere in cyberspace book, or found in any other "exciting" new electronic format that might happen to come along.

Completely free of keys, buttons, passwords, links, bytes, cookies, corruption, cyber space, piracy, downloads, uploads, buffering, backspacing, crashes, screen glare, torrents, data loss, file theft, brownouts, blackouts, frozen screens – and can never be deleted. What a concept. Just open it and read.

by

Paul Tice

THE BOOK TREE
San Diego, California

ISBN 978-1-58509-139-3

Cover layout by
Atulya Berube

Note: The views and opinions expressed in this book do not necessarily reflect those of the
publishing company.

Published by
The Book Tree
P O Box 16476
San Diego, CA 92176

www.thebooktree.com

We provide fascinating and educational products to help awaken the public to new ideas and
information that would not be available otherwise.
Call 1 (800) 700-8733 for our FREE BOOK TREE CATALOG.

Dedicated to

Traditional books
and those who love them

Also by Paul Tice

Shadow of Darkness, Dawning of Light: The Awakening of Human Consciousness in the 21st Century and Beyond

Triumph of the Human Spirit: The Greatest Acheivements of the Human Soul and How Its Power Can Change Your Life

That Old-Time Religion: The Story of Religious Foundations, with Jordan Maxwell and Dr. Alan Albert Snow

Jumpin' Jehovah: Exposing the Atrocities of the Old Testament God, 3rd edition

Mysteries Explored: The Search for Human Origins, UFOs, and Religious Beginnings, with Jack Barranger

A Booklet of Meaningful Quotes

CONTENTS

Special Note...6

Preface...7

Acknowledgments and Note to the Reader.......................8

Foreword..9

Introduction..11

Technology Overkill...19

The Case for Printed Books...27

E-book Limitations...47

The Post-Literate Society..95

Public Libraries...103

Newspapers...109

Summary...119

Special Note

This book was made for human readers. Not designed for Androids, Psions, Symbians, Kobos, Droids, JooJoos, Nooks, Archos, Rocketfish, Mobipockets, Kindles, iPods, iPads, Eee-pads, or pee-pads (for dogs). Not made for Microsoft Readers, Alex Readers, Arghos Readers, Palm OS Readers, DNL Readers, Apabi Readers, Nexus Sevens, Librettos, Cybooks, Pocket PCs, Windows Slates or Mobile Readers, Moby Tablets, BlackPads, WindPads, or any other non-human, non-conscious, semi-intelligent device. If you are a person, this book was meant for you.

PREFACE

This book is going against the grain of technology and the direction books are taking. For many reasons, the e-book is here to stay. They save a lot of space and it has been said that e-books create a bigger profit margin for publishers. Maybe that is why few books with this viewpoint have been published. So why was it done? It's simple. I love books. Real books. And so do millions of other people. Hopefully, this includes you. But in recent times, the world of books and reading has begun to shift more toward e-books.

After decades of trying, and with little results, e-books have finally broken through and are here to stay. They offer another avenue for readers to access information, for publishers to publish, and another way for writers to bring their messages to the public. This book, however, will remain as a paper book and only as a paper book. Its purpose is to remind everyone of a long-standing, cherished tradition rather than trying to launch an "attack" on e-books. I like e-books. But I love normal ones. This particular publisher has e-books available and will no doubt expand their offerings, just like everyone else. It is a great, additional outlet that every publisher should engage in – but without losing sight of the legacy and value of the book in its original form. Thank you for buying this book and supporting this particular format.

ACKNOWLEDGMENTS

Thanks to writer Jane Belanger for allowing the reproduction of her "Off the Cuff" column from the July 14, 2011 issue of the San Diego Reader, where four random people were asked, "Books of e-reader?" I would also like to thank editor Jim Holman from the Reader for putting me in touch with Jane and extending additional, official permission from his publication. Thanks also to the four respondents for their honest answers in the column – Katie McCanna, Juan-Carlos Cerda, Jesse Valadez and Terry Tyler.

A NOTE TO THE READER

If technology has improved – or will improve – to negate any of the critical points brought forth in this edition, I extend my apologies. I am not perfect, but have done my best, with the information available, to share facts and evidence and to express my opinions based on them. People are hard at work to mimic real books in every conceivable way, and to improve upon them (if you consider that possible). The knowledge and opinions I've shared do not attempt to mislead, but to inform and educate. The goal is to present the continued value of physical books, which have been perfected over many centuries. At the same time, I encourage people to read and educate themselves with e-books if it turns out they would otherwise not read anything at all. As with everyone, using electronic devices is a personal preference. Being critical of e-books serves no purpose if it prevents people from reading. Continue to read. Beyond that, the goal of this work is to remind you, the reader, about the value and joy of books in their original form.

FOREWORD

People and books have had a very long and personal relationship. With the advent of electronic books, it is time to remind you of this relationship and it's enduring value. When someone or something becomes a normal fixture in our lives, it often becomes easy to take them for granted and start searching for "alternatives." This is what has happened with books.

If a book could talk, what would it say about all this new technology? What if it was this book? The Introduction to this book comes from the book itself – communicating to you in the personal way we have experienced from them for centuries. This is not to say that e-books fail to do this. They just fail to do it as effectively, as you will see.

We owe an amazing debt to the book. It has changed history more than any other learning tool. An equal appreciation is due to the printing press, because without it, books would have never reached the public to any effective degree. The printing press has been recognized as the one thing, more than any other innovation, which has brought us out of ignorance and taught us to think for ourselves. We have been allowed to share information and educate ourselves far beyond anything that was previously possible. A tradition has been established between people and books. Books can change people's lives as much as direct events, because the exposure to *knowledge* can change entire mindsets and ways of thinking. The impact of books can go beyond the events experienced in people's lives, because knowledge – good, meaningful knowledge – stays with you.

Today, electronic gadgets driven by the desire for profits are being pushed on to the public in an effort to replace the long-standing tradition of printed books. It is mentioned by those selling these devices that these gadgets are simply an alternative way to access information in books effectively. It is "progress."

To a certain extent this is true. But if the makers of e-book devices had their way, they would completely displace books with their new technology and think nothing of it. More than one e-book executive has expressed this shallow notion as a clear goal of their company, without considering much of what will be shared in this book.

The book – the physical paper version – is *not* dead. The following Introduction was written from the book's perspective – from its point of view. Books have talked to people in important ways for centuries; now it is time for one to talk to you in yet another important way. About its contribution. Its true value. The debt you may owe it. And it's survival. Please allow this book to speak to you, on behalf of all books.

Following the Introduction, things will resume from a normal perspective.

INTRODUCTION

Hello. I'm a book. Remember me?

Due to the explosion of technological devices relating to "books," I think it's time that you and I had a chat.

The first thing I need to ask is, What on Earth are you doing? Are you people crazy? The further you move away from simplicity, the more you needlessly complicate your lives.

Your technology, which is supposed to make your lives easier, forces you into spending extra time and money that you could otherwise save.

Look at me. I've been around for centuries.

Some of you believe that you don't need me anymore. Because you love to *complicate things*. It keeps you busy. And as long as you are busy (rather than efficient), you are happy.

The simplest things that are still around have lasted so long because they work. But if you dress something up, modernize it, add some bells and whistles to *complicate it*, and make it look important, there's a good chance people will accept it and buy it. Today's general rule is to put anything up against a wall, throw some technology at it and if it happens to stick, market it like crazy. There's money to be made.

Professional marketers are paid to convince you that you need these things – the newest gadgets that will send you down a diversionary path.

As a result, you no longer respect tradition. Or simplicity. I represent these things.

Please respect me.

I have things of value. You have forgotten some of them in your mad rush toward "progress." I am not complicated.

For example, you cannot erase me or lose me if your computer crashes.

Also, you don't need "keys" to bring me up or find me.

I'm easy to find because I am a real, physical object. You can see me in the room because I am not a phantom, hiding in the invisible memory of a gadget.

You do not have to stare into a screen to read me. Don't you do enough of that already? Save it for TV.

If you happen to lose me, you will not lose your entire library along with me.

I can have many different owners.

I can show wear and age – *just like you* – which gives me character.

You can't delete me by mistake.

I am not cold and mechanical. I am warm, special and unique.

For some reason, people always prefer me on a cold night next to the fire. It is a centuries-old tradition, which would lose its charm with a cold electronic device. Nothing can replace reading a book near the fireplace on a quiet winter night. In my opinion weird devices, rather than a book, should be used as "kindling."

I have an identity of my own. If I share my physical space with hundreds of other titles in one tiny little electronic device or computer then, no matter how good I am, I become just another number – one out of many – easily lost, forgotten or ignored. My knowledge is not so accessible because when I am out of sight, I'm out of mind. That's what would happen to most books, over time, if converted and stored in this way. Knowledge would be lost. Society will continue to be "dumbed down," because people will not bother themselves as much with things *that cannot be seen*. I become merely a figment of your imagination, hidden inside a gadget when you don't want me around.

I look *good* on a shelf. People forget that.

Feel me. Feel my texture. It is a wonderful tactile sensation. This is what a book feels like. Now put me down and just look at a screen with words on it (or imagine it, if one is not around). It is a much different experience. Many prefer physical contact with me. The power of touch is a very connective and emotional experience. There is a deeper emotional connection to a physical book. When you are not able to touch a book and turn it's physical pages as you read, it is almost like depriving yourself of physical contact with your mate, and replacing it with your imagination. It doesn't work so well.

Smell me. Smell the pages. I am very real. This is what a book smells like. Older books smell even better. I am not a ghostly thing that disappears and comes back again when you "boot" me up. Don't make me into a ghost. I deserve better. And I don't like to be "booted," either.

My publisher will not make me into a ghost. You can only get me in this form. Why? Because you really GET me.

Can your standard little hand held e-book reader or Internet-accessing phone show a page this size, or enlarge words while maintaining a smooth flow and readability as you read from it's tiny screen? Can it? NO, it cannot!

If a little hand held device *can* enlarge text, what is the point? You would only be able to read a few words at a time. Okay, so the iPad and similar sized tablets can do it, but they are the same size as most books. So that works. But with them, however, the tactile sensation of a true book is lost. There is no replacement for holding a paper book and turning each page yourself, rather than clicking a button and watching some kind of fantasy graphic that *simulates* the experience. Would you rather play your favorite sport, or play a simulated computer game?

And for those who like to take notes on end pages, or who like to physically write in the margins, there is no way to do this in many e-books. A few devices allow it, but it is not as easy and more cumbersome to write on something that is not a physical object. To their credit, you can highlight or underline easily with some of them. Taking physical notes, however, is important to many researchers and students in all kinds of subjects, including technical books, medical texts and with books on any subject, depending on the reader.

The Bible

The most published book in the western world is the Bible, so I need to remind you of my appearance in a religious and physical context. The Bible is very personal. Being able to carry your Bible around is important. You seem to lose that special "connection" with some kind of electronic device. Sitting in church and being asked to open your Bible to a certain chapter and verse, and then watching people open little electronic devices with all kinds of little "bleeps" and "bloops" going off in the room, instead of using a real book constitutes outright blasphemy to "old school" Christians. It just isn't right. The Bible was created by man in the form of a real *book*. It was never meant to become invisible – and stuffed into an electronic gadget. Just because something is new does not mean it is better, or that it is the right thing to do. You are being told it is the right thing to do because certain companies want your money. Donate that money to your church, and read a normal Bible for God's sake.

Why I'm Better

As a physical book, you only need to buy me once and if you treat me right, I can last over 100 years. Try *that* with any of these new-fangled electronic devices, which become obsolete at an alarming pace. New e-book formats continue to evolve or be created, and will always force you to convert or update your files constantly. It is also clear that most types of reading devices will be obsolete quite soon. It's the same with computer software. It always needs to be updated every few years and that will never change, either. Current e-book readers will become outdated relatively soon, as compared to the long life of a book. You might pay less for an e-book, but in the long run, all of you will pay more. My traditional, trusted form does not need updates. On rare occasions, my author might add valuable new information to my content, but that is a different kind of "update" (not an electronic format or entirely new operating system). In general, just buy me once, without updates, and put me in a good visible place for when you need me again. You can then reach for me and open me *with your hands*.

When you buy me you hold me in your hands. I'm real! If you own an e-book, where is it? It is *not* a tangible product. The words on a physical page have substance, and you can feel them, and smell them. But what do you say about an electronic file? "Excuse me, but can you pass me those bytes?" And when the file is closed, it becomes even *more* elusive. If it's not "open" and on your screen, how do you even know that it exists? It is just a figment of your imagination. You better go look and see if your e-books are still there. They could have been erased by a software glitch or electronic surge about twenty minutes ago and you could have lost everything.

How can you give an e-book as a gift? You cannot unwrap it as a gift. It's completely invisible until you open it (on a computerized device). With me, you can wrap me up in beautiful paper and top in off with a bow. With an e-book you would have to send it in an email – *which is also invisible until it's opened.* Will those who receive it say, "How cute!" or "How thoughtful."? NO! Because giving an e-book is not cute *or* thoughtful when you get right down to it – because it is a cold and distant act. It's *invisible* for God's sake, so it's practically an insult. Virtually anything makes a better gift. Especially me.

Some people think ghosts are real, but ghosts are not part of this physical world. Even if they do happen to exist, they don't really *belong* here. They are merely phantoms. E-books are nothing but phantoms. They are not real books. They are "ghost books." You cannot hold one physically in your hand. You can hold the device that has "captured" one, and delude yourself into thinking that you have it, and it's real, but how do you really know it's there? You cannot hold the book up or examine it – because it's not a book! It's just a bunch of electronic bytes that are masquerading as a book. And you accept it as a "book" because you've been *told* that it's one. And you believe it. You have been brainwashed. It is not a book. *I* am a book.

If you were looking for the services of a person and someone told you they had a ghost to do the job for you, for a little less money, would you buy into that? Of course not! But in the case of books, you *are* buying into it. People are parting with their hard earned money in exchange for e-books and the little square "coffins" – or electronic devices – that hold these ghostly phantoms. Proponents of e-books are crowing with hope that the standard book is dead, but in reality it is the e-book that is far more "dead" than a real book ever will be. I will never die. I give *life* to a room.

When you walk into a room that has a beautiful library, owned by a true book lover, the books look impressive. And they tell a story, just by glancing at them, about the person who owns them. You can learn a great deal about a person by browsing in their library. Someone's personal files are usually treated more privately and people in general are not likely to invite you to browse through their personal files, which are far colder and less inviting anyway. When someone prefers to own e-books instead, it reveals just as much about the person who thinks he "owns" them. But he will have to go look for them in some computerized folder or on a gadget first, because they're *invisible*.

I will always be here for you, right in plain sight. You cannot turn me off. I don't operate with electricity. I am only dependent upon your eyes, not a cute gadget. You don't need to depend on the manipulation of technology to access my information. You only need to see. That's all. If you can see, then we're in business. These new-fangled LCD screens, which most e-readers have, cannot be seen well from an angle. Normal books like me can be read well from extreme angles by comparison. Unless you have bad vision, you do not need to put me right up in front of your face just to experience what I have to say. Nor do you need to charge a device, download a file or attempt to brighten or manipulate my screen. Just look at me. Why do you people always have to complicate things? I'm a *book*, for God's sake!

If it gets really hot or cold and you leave your little book reader out, exposed to elements, guess what? You have *fried* your device and lost your invisible files. But with me, so what? I don't care. Leave me in the sun. My spine might fade a little if I'm near a window for months on end, but other than that, I'm no worse off. You will be happy with me, and not resort to jumping up and down in anger; nor will you have to figure out how to come up with the money to replace your device and all of the files that were lost.

Gutenberg, the inventor of the printing press, is rolling over in his grave right now. I cannot see him doing this, but because I, as a book, have been imbued with his spirit, I know this is true. He is trying to get back out and warn you because so much of what he gave you is being taken away by small, lit up screens and slick business people who are trying to convince you to squint at them. And what for? So an inventive "techno-geek" who contracted with a gadget company can get rich. And what are you getting in return? You are not getting real books at all. They are *simulated* books. Why should you settle for a simulation of something when you can have the real thing?

I am not a hidden file. Thank you for having bought me, for I am truly real.

Chapter One

Technology Overkill

Is new technology always good? Some of the additional technology, other than books, will be covered in this chapter because it is important to see what society has done with it. It is helpful to look at the big picture of technology in order to get a better perspective on e-books.

Technology is meant to increase the power and range of our control over the world around us. Therefore, it should make things easier for us. That is its ultimate purpose. But as technology increases, so does its complexity – and complexity creates snags, problems, headaches, lost time, *additional expense* and frustration. We have reached the point in most areas of society where we need to revert to the old philosophical maxim of Occam's Razor – where the simplest answer to a problem is usually the best answer. New technology is often not simpler, but is "dressed up" to look better and thereby attract new customers. With e-books, you now have an extra device to operate, coming in between you and the direct experience of a physical book, with extra keys and buttons to operate in order to access the material. Some people like this – but it does not necessarily make it a better experience. And it is clearly not as simple.

All this new technology is just another offshoot of the neurosis of mankind. For example, politics is necessary in order for us to live in a just and fair society. But we don't know when to stop. Politicians needs jobs, the human mind never stops and relaxes, so to make themselves "useful," politicians continue to create new rules and regulations – whether we need them or not. They tell us we need them because it justifies their jobs. It often results in lost freedoms for the people who elected these clowns – creating the exact opposite of what we wanted in the first place, which is fairness and an easier life. The extra regulations, fees and taxes we must put up with have reached insane proportions.

We have entangled ourselves with our own "brilliance." Things are so immensely complicated that little gets done. More activity takes place with the red tape and entanglements that allow investors to get their cut of your money than with actually making life easier – which was the original plan to begin with. We have done this to ourselves not only with technology, but also in the fields of medicine, legal areas and with food. The medical and pharmaceutical cartels are huge rackets which have turned into big business, now focused more on making money than with healing and helping those in need. The more you research it – or are one of those who have experienced this first-hand, through needless suffering – the more you will understand the truth of this statement.

With food, we now think we are smarter than nature – creating designer foods in the laboratory (GMOs – Genetically Modified Organisms), patenting them in order to make money and replacing *real* food with these imposters – similar to the way we have replaced real books with fake, electronic cyber books. The original sales pitch was to find a way to reduce hunger, but numerous studies have proven that GMO crops do not increase yields. Control of the seeds makes millions for companies like Monsanto, however, and monopolizes the control of food because the seeds do not reproduce naturally. They must be bought every year by, in many cases, poor farmers. The effects on human health from long-term consumption have never been tested. Too much money has been invested in creating these "franken-foods," and these huge companies need to turn a quick profit for their investors and cannot wait 20 years to do it. They want it now. In the meantime, we are all the guinea pigs. Most food is now genetically modified, but they do not have to legally reveal this on labels in the U. S. as of this writing (so they don't). In Europe, however, it is the law.

What complicates things is that the huge multi-billion dollar Gates Foundation, owned by Microsoft mogul Bill Gates, is an investor in Monsanto's GMOs (not so good), but also an investor in saving newspapers and news organizations (good). Most of these news organizations now refuse to bite the hand that feeds them, and will not report anything negative on genetically modified foods. The world has enough good, *real* food to eliminate hunger but the logistics to get it to the needy is what has always been lacking. If a coordinated transportation system was invested in the problem would be solved, but there is no incentive for profit in this. In 2010 Gates bought 500,000 shares in Monsanto, valued at about $23 million. Please see the article "Bill Gates, Monsanto and Eugenics: How One of the World's Wealthiest Men is Actively Promoting Corporate Takeover of Agriculture," by Ethan Huff at www.bibliotecapleyades.net/sociopolitica/sociopol_win-micro-gates17.htm. See also the interesting piece on Bill Gates at http://articles.mercola.com/sites/articles/archive/2012/03/04/clueless-fabrication-on-gmo.aspx by Dr. Mercola.

The point of all this is that there is a *pattern* here. Yes, this book is about e-books, but the same dysfunctional pattern has spread itself into many areas of our culture. I have mentioned a few of these other areas just so you can see the bigger picture – and see what is really going on here. We don't know when to leave things well enough alone when we happen to have it good. A new, exciting feature is always the "bait," but the baggage that goes along with it, meant to make others rich at your expense, is never worth the trade-off for most people. *You are sold the sizzle, but never get the steak.* The sad part is that most people are convinced that the sizzle really is the steak – and they are satisfied. Pick up a *real book*, compare it to an e-book, and see what I am saying.

We always have to make things "better," but it always gets to a point where things become way too complicated. We think we can control the complications – and usually do a pretty good job of it. When you look back to the simplicity that once existed, it often looks better than the extra baggage we get saddled with. Some people refer to these times as "the good old days." This means that simpler days, filled with more *freedom*, will never be experienced again. We've complicated things so much that we have enslaved ourselves. We have become so obligated to so many different vested interests, that there is no way to ever turn back. Of all things, this is truer with technology than with most everything else.

This neurosis of complicating everything may well account for the huge numbers of psychological disorders experienced in our society today. As things "progress," more and more people can't take it anymore and become defective on some level. Or they just "snap." So many different things are all grabbing at your wallet, demanding your attention and cash, whether it is a legitimate enterprise or not. You must jump through so many hoops to get anything done these days, there is very little free time left for you to actually enjoy yourself. We have created too many extra rules and regulations for our own "protection," and many of them require fees. As a result, any extra money that you would use for your free time (if you have any) is also lacking.

We've somehow tricked ourselves into believing that we have created a "better world," with most of it centering on new technology. But the newest technology has reached a point where much of it is not needed. The companies that create this technology need the money from sales, and you as their prisoner – once you buy into the product. But you, as a consumer, do not really need most of it. The complications, in most cases, outweigh the benefits. For example, many things are carefully tested, designed and built to break or fall apart shortly after the standard warranty on the product runs out. Or, in the case of software, upgrades must continue to be made. I call these "intentional complications," and they are far more common than you could ever imagine. It was important 40 to 50 years ago to make a high quality product that would last a lifetime. In post World War II society it was important to show the world that America made the very best of everything – things that would last a lifetime. But it didn't take long for companies to realize that there was no money in creating the best quality. The need for constant upgrades or replacements now dominates everything, including technology. With e-books and e-readers, these intentional complications are both evident and hidden. This book will cover them all.

Proponents of new technology are trying to convince you that all these new advances will make your experience "better" in many different areas. For a random example, let's look at professional baseball. It is now possible to replace all of the umpires on the field with technology that is capable of determining outcomes with more accuracy. Accuracy to the point of centimeters is not that important and continually stopping a game to dissect it is annoying. Too much control with technology ruins the spontaneity and fluidity of sports and also removes the joy from many other simple things in life. When watching a game on television you can now see, through a superimposed "box" over the strike zone, a more accurate view of balls and strikes. This could be easily integrated into the game to determine balls and strikes. Along with various camera angles and slow-motion replay at all the bases, the on-field umpires could be a thing of the past – or, at most, used as "puppets" to keep the old look of the game. Would people want this?

Some would, but would this still be baseball? No it would not. Gone would be the umpires shouting, "Play ball!" at the start of each game, booming out the called strikes, the dramatic "safe" or "out" sign on close plays – and sometimes the resulting arguments of these plays. Gone would be the dramatic ejections of players or managers, and things like brushing off home plate, keeping the supply of balls properly moving, and the overall personal warmth and effect of having umpires – all this would be gone. It would not be baseball anymore. It would be colder and more distant like e-books. And when things get out of control with bench-clearing brawls, which can happen from time to time, the umpires are actually needed to break them up. Without them, both sides could cause greater injury to each other, and the fans could get involved easier, which has been known to happen in some cases. Fights could become a massive, confusing free-for-all. This is exactly what's happened with this current e-book "revolution." Numerous gadgets and e-book formats are fighting for attention and control. The point? Trying to control things with technology – just because you can – is not always a good thing.

Read a normal book. Right now, dozens of e-book formats are fighting it out. Stand aside and let them do it. Everyone has rushed the "field," creating their own interpretations, supporting a format of their own or of some other company's that will make them money, trying to beat their opponents into submission. It has become chaotic and confusing. Unless you are up to speed with all this craziness, it's hard to tell the difference between what is software and what is hardware; what each item does compared to others; what is dependable; what will stand the test of time or become obsolete or unpopular; which will enhance or destroy your investment of time in learning how to operate the device or it's software. You have (among others), the i-book, Cybook, nook book, Kobo, Kindle, pdf, opf, EPUB, Plucker, HTML, TealDoc, Mobipocket, eReader, Arghos Reader, Microsoft Reader, DNL Reader, Apabi Reader, SSReader, TomeRaider, TEI, XMDF, CSS, Compressed HM, RAR, TAR, ACE, ZIP, IEC 62448, DAISY, DjVu, XML, ICARUS, iLiad, eStick, Open eBook, Newton eBook, Broadband eBook, Multimedia eBook, FictionBook PocketBook, Rocketbook, Flip Book, or you must learn how to access files floating somewhere in a cloud out there in cyberspace. What happened to the good old-fashioned book? If this particular book appears in *any form* other than as a traditional paper book, it has been put there by a thief and is a violation of copyright law. It is being presented in this way only, in order to make a point.

People often say they relaxed at home by curling up with a good book. What they mean is a real book. I am sure you have not heard it said that someone curled up with their e-book reader and if they did, were they really all that cozy? Maybe it's possible, but something about it just does not seem to work. The "warmth" is, and always will be, found with a real book.

There are new technological devices that you can hook up to your TV and simulate real events. You can go bowling, play tennis and engage in all kinds of "activities" by moving your body to simulate the actions necessary to engage in these sports, and watch the "outcome" on your TV screen. This is supposed to be fun. But here's a better idea. If you want to do any of these activities, then *go out and actually do them!* What are you, idiots? The levels of obesity in people are higher than ever, so you should be concerned with exercising properly and taking care of your health. If you are disabled, then these programs are perfect for you. Buy them and use them. If you are not disabled and use them in place of real events, then you are either pitifully lazy or a complete idiot – one that has fallen for a slick marketing campaign that has convinced you that you actually need products that replace genuine, healthy activity. Do not allow technology to rule your life and replace genuine events (and genuine books) with counterfeits – *cheap, simulated counterfeits.*

Chapter Two

The Case for Printed Books

Sometimes the devices used for reading e-books can multi-task. One of them is called texting, which is the ability to type on an incredibly tiny "keyboard" in order to send electronic text messages to your friends over your network. There have been deaths of many young people who were texting while they were driving. In all of the terrible reports that have come out, letting you know of these tragedies, it's often been revealed that those who died were typing text – but it is quite possible that some of them were trying to read it as well.

Those who love to read have the opportunity to access text messages and/or books while they are driving, due to the portability of these devices. College students cramming for a test can now "study" while they drive to class – which allows more time for that all-important party the night before. Because of this sort of thing, you should prefer to read a normal book and not involve yourself in the endangerment of yourself or your children. Please keep normal books in your life.

There are those who will argue that an e-book will last longer than a printed book because it can never be "damaged" or subjected to wear and tear, or physical abuse. But the fact is that, on average, the shelf life of a physical book exceeds the life of an e-book. That is a fact. Hardware and software become outdated every few years and can make your e-book version or it's reading device obsolete in a relatively short period, whereby a printed book can last for many decades – sometimes over a century. An e-book reader's battery will become completely drained in a few years, eventually requiring replacement for additional cost, and power problems may put e-books stored on it in jeopardy.

Documents get corrupted over time. Software can do all kinds of crazy things including freezing, crashing, becoming corrupted, disappearing, and delivering all kinds of unexpected malfunctions that you could never imagine with a standard, everyday book. The e-book hardware itself, due to its electronic and computer-like nature, can suddenly develop strange "symptoms" that may require the help of a technician to solve. This not only may shorten the life of your e-books, but could suddenly make you short on cash as well.

If you drop a printed book it might get dented or scuffed a little, but if you drop an e-book reader it can suffer far more expensive damage due to the sensitivity of the item. Gadgets have all kinds of little moving things that make them susceptible to damage, whereby a real book has only pages. You don't have to protect a normal book from extreme heat or cold, but an e-book reader can be totally destroyed by temperature fluctuations. Water damage is undesirable in a normal book and can certainly happen, but the same amount of water contact to an e-book reader can be potentially more harmful, causing the reader to become inoperable or causing the complete loss of data for multiple books rather than one. Normal books can still be lost due to complete submersion in water, but do not react so severely to physical impacts or at all to power surges, extreme temperatures or electromagnetic pulses.

Smaller e-book readers are not good for youngsters because children tend to lose things and these gadgets are expensive. Books in general are bigger, thicker and less likely to be lost. Children are more visually oriented so smaller screens don't work. Pictures play a big role in the early educational, reading process. Matching pictures often go with the text, showing children what is being referred to. This is a very important facet of early learning. Small gadgets lack not only the size, but also the resolution to display these images properly for children. Bigger e-readers in the form of tablets are available that solve some of these issues, but there is the increased cost of the unit to consider and the problem of eyestrain from a computerized screen, even in the improved versions of these devices.

Young children love pop-up books that have three-dimensional characters and objects that "pop up" from the pages when you turn them. This keeps children directly engaged in the story and is not possible with flat screens. There is a current a movement for parents to use real books with their children instead of electronic devices. This is because there is an element of *discovery* when a child physically turns a page – especially when there are pictures on the other side. Physically turning a page to uncover something constitutes a discovery by involving the reader far more than by pushing a button or clicking a mouse. We are distancing our children from life with our "convenient" electronic devices. In fact, e-books distance everyone from the adventure of reading, no matter what your age might be.

Books with larger diagrams, technical layouts or genealogies also work poorly on e-readers with smaller footprints than a normal page. E-books have solved a convenience problem for those who want quick and easy access to information. They serve this purpose so well that in this increasingly fast-paced society they will no doubt continue to do so. But for those who want to spend time in deeper study, reflection or relaxing with a book, as people have done for centuries, the use of e-books falls short.

Printed books create a more emotional experience with the reader because you are more directly engaged in the reading experience and therefore, with the material. A computerized screen, whether big or small, is a "go-between." It distances you by an extra step from a physical book. Printed books are more tactile and direct. Scrolling and jumping around are required in the computerized world, creating extra work in order to access the material. Your "flow" is often lost, with extra hoops to jump through so you can have the "convenience" of reading with a device. Print, however, is solid and dependable – you will not lose your information by hitting a wrong button or mistakenly scroll in the wrong direction and become lost. E-book users get lost easily, with less reference points, but with a real book it is almost impossible. You can stay focused and digest your book without distractions, and thereby engage the material in a more emotional way. *Print moves you without moving.* Scrolling and jumping around is always a distraction.

People often comment on having the tactile sensation of holding a real book. This is important to many. The physical feel of the paper, binding and cover of the original printed work somehow satisfies people far more than an electronic device or staring at a screen, which is colder and more "distant." E-books only give you the words from the pages, nothing more. However, a good author or publisher always considers the size and layout of the book they wish to create, which helps to convey their message in a better way. Will the cover art and/or the words fit better on a 5.5 x 8.5 inch footprint, or will it display better at 6 x 9 or even at 8.5 x 11? What kind of art and interior pictures will appeal most to the target audience? The larger the artwork, the more impact it will have – and often times, e-readers are not large enough to accommodate sizable art, or have the resolution to display it properly.

Will a hardcover format work better than a standard soft cover? If so, how can the reader be intrigued and informed with additional information on the inner sleeves of the dust jacket? After all, with e-books, all you get is the interior text – any "bonus" information is usually excluded. Should the book be bound with a plastic comb binding, or ring binding, like a cookbook or technical manual, so that the book will stay open on a certain page for reference purposes? These are just some of the questions you can ask in relation to real books, and many answers that you create are clear *advantages* over the e-book.

Book covers can be made out of countless materials or fabrics. Older books sometimes used leather and even today some Bibles continue to use it or have switched to faux leather. Format is also important. Small gifts books are very popular, about 4 x 6 inches or 3 x 5, in landscape or traditional mode – but they would lose their impact as e-books. Physical books continue to benefit from different looks and feels, which e-books files encased in hard plastic devices do not have.

People also love physical bookmarks, which don't work with e-books and become unnecessary. Some publishers make bookmarks that match their particular titles, which is a nice touch. Bookmarks of all kinds spread great messages and can advertise the publisher, author, any worthy cause, or the store where the book was bought. Some share meaningful quotes, poetry or philosophical knowledge on their bookmarks – gentle reminders to live a better life or care more for others. Nice artwork can be found and appreciated on bookmarks. Most are paper, some are plastic, some are fabric – and some even glow in the dark. Bibles and other nicely published works often include built-in cloth ribbons or cloth strips that serve beautifully as bookmarks. The best bookmarks of all can be things from the natural world found by the reader and used for that purpose. Some of the things that have been found in second-hand books include four-leaf clovers, feathers of various colors and sizes, flowers and autumn leaves. Try using *these* with an e-book!

Real books can come with interesting extras or "accessories." Bonus foldout maps or charts often come with historical or other reference books, which would be virtually impossible to view on a single page from an e-reader or computer. Related CDs or DVDs are sometimes added into the backs of books, fitted into a sleeve on the inside of the back cover. Sure, an e-book could provide you with an Internet link to the same material, but whenever you want to access it, you need to have the book "open." It is claimed that all kinds of interactive data will be coming with e-books when the technology becomes more sophisticated, but the question remains how far publishers really want to go to prepare their books – especially when the initial research shows that consumers are not much interested in an abundance of links or interactive visuals. Making a book into a Hollywood production isn't really how people envision books, and it's too early to try and convince people that it's a good idea. Give me a normal physical book and I'm happy.

An e-book is good for letting a reader pop in and gather quick information. The screens support quick reading or gathering a few references. Based on general opinion, they do not allow the reader to experience sensations that support reading for pleasure, and to be alone with the author's thoughts. Many people strongly believe that an e-reading device is actually a *distraction* and an *impediment* to this larger purpose.

What follows is an article called "Off the Cuff," that appeared in The San Diego Reader newspaper on July 14, 2011. Random people off the street were asked:

Books or e-reader?

Books! They don't smell the same and you can't write in them and it's just not the same experience if it's not on paper. Maybe if they came out with a waterproof e-reader I could get into it. Like, reading in the bath's kind of irritating. So, maybe if they had a waterproof one – with Smell-a-vision so that old book smell just shoots right out of there. Aromatherapy reader.
— Katie McCanna, Marketing, Normal Heights

It has to be a book. I've got the Amazon Kindle app on my phone, but I much prefer to have the actual physical book in my hand.

— Juan-Carlos Cerda, Respiratory Therapist, Chula Vista

Books. I've tried an e-reader, but I don't like it. It's too black-and-white.

— Jesse Valadez, Distributor, National City

Books. I just don't like the idea of reading off a machine. I want to be a page-turner.

— Terry Tyler, Student, Central San Diego

The first major hurdle in acquiring an e-book reader is cost. An e-book reader costs far more than a single book. It is true that many e-books cost a little less than a new physical book, so you are presented with the illusion of getting the e-reader's investment back, but other hidden costs and essential upgrades will remove this factor. Sometimes, e-books can cost just as much as their print versions, depending on the title. Most of the time, however, an e-book will cost less than a new paper one. This includes free versions of some public domain books. When you put a lesser price on knowledge, however, people tend to think of it as being unimportant. Even if they do buy or download the e-book, they often store it away, out of sight, and never get around to reading it. In cases like this you get what you pay for – nothing (or close to it). A real book, however, stays visible on a shelf, reminding you of the knowledge it contains. Today, knowledge has become less important than electronic profits, falling victim to countless individuals and companies that are flooding the market with digital books, continually under-bidding each other in the quest for electronic "riches." As a result, the knowledge accessed in books continues to be diminished. And the knowledge *gleaned* from books continues to be diminished. People tend to read a paper book from cover to cover more often than they do a digital book. In general, people scan through an e-book for bits of information or search through them using search functions and even linking – and jumping to – other data on the Internet, thereby leaving their book behind. Being distracted comes easier with e-books because diversionary technology is continually at the user's fingertips. With information presented in this way, it is no surprise that the attention spans of young people are almost non-existent compared to what was practiced a few decades ago, and that ADD (Attention Deficit Disorder) is more prevalent in society than ever before. Instead of changing people's habits to eliminate the problem, however, children are often prescribed drugs while they continue with their distraction-based behaviors.

Book Versions to Consider

Purchasing a used version of a paper book can often get you the title in the cheapest way possible. Some public domain e-books are available for free, but the quality can be horrendous. Many e-books found online have been scanned through OCR (optical character recognition), and never edited. OCR is not perfect, especially in identifying letters and characters from older printed books, which always had minor imperfections. For example, OCR scanners will often translate a 'c' and an "l" appearing together (cl) as the single letter "d." This is just one example. Hundreds of scanning errors appear in these "free" e-books, which should be *edited*, before sending them out into the world. But some companies are more concerned with quantity rather than quality and are only in the book business not out of love for books, but to make as much money as possible. Many such companies have also produced these books as printed physical books, and charge good money for them. These people and companies who put out non-edited, scanned books, and charge for them, do not love books or care about them at all. Money is their only concern. Giving you an inferior product does not matter to them and there are many, many companies out there doing this, – *polluting* the book world with their garbage. Do yourself a favor. Do not patronize these companies.

The publisher of this book has reprinted older books for many years without using OCR in almost every case. The books appear exactly as they had years ago. The minor imperfections are still there, but at least they remain *readable*. When OCR is used on a title, one must take the time to edit it properly, without throwing it into the marketplace as a jumbled mess.

The point is, if you are trying to save money by buying cheaper versions of any book, whether it be an e-book or a printed book, *be careful*. Any book sourced from or available as an electronic version involves complications not found when using simpler printing techniques. *Just because it is new and uses great "technology" does not necessarily mean it's better.* People don't get that. Remember these words: The time will come when it will suddenly dawn on people how much real books are missed, and what a mistake has been made, and people will start returning to bookstores. It has already started to happen. But guess what? Most of these stores are *gone*.

The publisher's small, independent bookstore in San Diego has weathered the storm – still standing after giants like Borders, one of the biggest national book chains in the US, has fallen, among many other larger stores. The climate is clearly changing, and Book Tree may one day not have its bricks and mortar store, but for now it is still there. A few years ago no one would have ever imagined the demise of Borders Books and Music. Borders had over 600 stores in operation and employed over 30,000 people who all lost their jobs. With this competition gone, it has helped independent stores that have managed to hang on, to do slightly better at this point in time. Some people have realized that e-books are not giving them what is promised on a number of levels and, after looking deeper, have returned to the "normalcy" of traditional books. Who's to say how long this will last, however. Despite all the hype, there is a downside to e-books that people are beginning to notice. To some, e-books are a convenient answer but to others, it has been a passing fad. They tried it, may have even bought a device, but prefer a normal book when all is said and done.

Chinks in the e-book Armor

For most of the people in the world, the cost of an e-reader is too high. When people must watch their money, real books work out better every time. You never need a battery, software, or upgrades to your device, software or operating system. When looking for an affordable book, they can almost always turn to the used book market and get one for less than the cost of to an e-book (without having to buy an expensive reader). When they are done reading it, they can return to the used book market and sell it again. There is no such thing as a used e-book – they are completely non-existent. This means you cannot turn around and sell your e-book after you have finished reading it, in order to recoup some of your original costs. Most of the world prefers to buy used books at an affordable discount and – if you keep them in the same shape – it is possible for you to get your money back. This means if you are smart, you can read your books for free, or close to free, by using standard books instead of e-books.

Also, rare books can increase in value. Collectors who have held on to their books now have libraries of immense value. However, with e-books there is no investment value in having any electronic book whatsoever. They are totally useless as an investment. Nor do they have any artistic value, being nothing more than an invisible collection of bytes and data that suddenly appear when your gadget fires up and you open the file.

Cover art is not appreciated much in relation to e-books. It is often kept and displayed, but is not presented well, due to a flat, two-dimensional screen. And a collection of books – a small library in a home or office has an appealing look that many people desire. Some older books (and their modern reproductions) are beautiful in their craftsmanship and, in part, are intended to serve this purpose. There are some people who love the classic look of collectible books, and use them in a decorative sense to enhance the look of their home or office. For those who appreciate the decorative aspect of displaying books or if you love books in general, a must site to visit is www.bookshelfporn. com. You will see some amazing and inventive collections. Beyond having a certain look, older, rare books are collectible for their scarcity, condition and/or historical importance. Some of them are one of a kind (not possible with e-books). Signed copies by famous people including presidents, world leaders, sports stars and celebrities, can significantly increase the importance and value of any book. How can any such thing be possible with an e-book? A collectible e-book? With a digital signature? Forget it.

What about your average, every-day used book that happens to not be collectible? As mentioned, you can resell or trade in a used book when done with it and make some or all of your money back. In this respect an e-book is worthless. If you resell it on the Internet at retail, you could get most of your money back or can even make a profit. Or you could trade in your used books at a second hand store, which will provide some return on your investment. This in turn helps support used bookstores, which are wonderful places to visit and need your support to continue to exist. People often buy their used books on the Internet, but you must know exactly what you want and then search out the specific title before buying it. The shame of all this is that many younger people have never been in a used bookstore. A used bookstore can be a magical place. They need to be experienced, instead of substituting the experience for a cold and distant Internet search. You embark on an interesting adventure each time you visit a used bookstore. You never know what you will find on every visit, and often leave with a new discovery or treasure – something you never knew existed and may enrich your life as a result.

The Internet book buying experience is cold and distant by comparison. Shopping in bookstores, especially used bookstores, is _incredibly fun!_ Yet the Internet has put hundreds of these places out of business because many people are too lazy to support a physical store. They only buy what they've been told to buy and search only for what they want ahead of time, rather than being open to new discoveries. Browsing in an actual store and on the Internet are two entirely different things. In a bookstore you can immediately walk away with a big stack of books from one location, without waiting – and you don't have to pay for shipping. Some will argue that cheaper prices are to be found on the Internet, but often times these same people forget about the shipping costs _and_ you cannot inspect the quality of the books over the Internet as you can do in a real store. As has been often discovered, you cannot take a seller's word for what the quality is, and what is considered "very good" to a seller may not be "very good" to you at all.

You might ask, Why not get e-books instead? After all, e-books also remove the cost of shipping and you get your "book" instantly, for a cheaper price. But that lesser cost disappears later, through clever, well thought out, long term obligations which are not clearly evident on the surface. And you cannot resell the book later, or trade it back in to a used bookstore for value. Your investment is totally dead once you've downloaded your ghost book. There's some kind of "loaning" technology surfacing now so you can share it in a limited way, but in a financial sense, your investment is dead. The e-book is not as alive or real like a paper book, and neither is your investment. The so-called book you have downloaded does not really exist, and neither does your investment value. It is all dead; the whole darn thing is deficient on a number of key levels, a big charade, and you are stuck with it. Unless, of course, you hit one button by mistake and delete the file.

This can happen because e-readers are small, mobile devices that get stuffed into pockets, backpacks and purses while bumping up against other items after being forgotten to be turned off – or they simply get turned on and activated during the traveling and bumping process.

When you buy a physical book in a physical store you know exactly what you are getting. You can see it, feel it, touch and smell it. It's not pretending to be something it is not. With this in mind, Book Business magazine, from July/August 2011, quotes a CBSNews.com article by Ysolt Usigan, which reports how spam has infiltrated e-books. In relation to Kindle's e-book self-publishing program, Usigan said, "These books are built using Private Label Rights that allow virtually anyone to post written works. Although it sounds like a great resource for aspiring authors... [it's] making it easier for spammers." When Usigan dug further, Internet marketing specialist Paul Wolfe told him, "One tactic involves copying a [top-selling e-book] and republishing it with new titles and covers...." Inside the book is just a bunch of spam offers. But the spam title is designed to show up in searches along with the real, best selling title, making it easy for shoppers to purchase the fake one. Unfortunately, spam has also infiltrated many different devices, including various e-book readers that can access the Internet.

E-readers and computer-like devices are often multi-functional in nature and are worth more money than a single book, so thieves are more likely to steal one than bother with a single paper book. And if this should happen, you can lose far more than a single book since the device can hold a few hundred – or even a few thousand – files. Sure, having one can be a positive aspect as well, saving space, but you will never, ever misplace hundreds of *real* books by forgetting a small device on the bus, or have someone steal them all in public – and conceal them from you – because you happened to look away or be distracted for a brief moment. As small as it is, your e-reader is a much larger target for theft than the same books in traditional form. The concept of using an Internet "cloud" can save you from losing your books, but it is unclear whether everyone is going to want this or bother with it – mainly because it still another step removed from a real book *and* from an actual downloadable and ownable e-book.

Clouds on the Internet

Some online e-book vendors can back up books for you in "digital lockers" or in a "cloud," should you ever have them lost or stolen. Some vendors are using these clouds exclusively, as the main form of access rather than as a backup. So you never own a book from a cloud, but must "rent" your e-book (or what you would be calling "your" e-book) from them. My opinion is that since you do not really "own" anything in a cloud, why bother with it? You can have access to it for a certain period of time and then it is gone. The general setup is the same as hard drive backup systems that have been offered to businesses for years. These e-book companies have thrown a collection of book files on a backup hard drive, given it a fancy new name, and voila! The "cloud" is born. With this in mind, why not go out and buy your *own* backup hard drive, instead of being hypnotized by some bells and whistles, and a neat new marketing ploy designed to take your money for something you can do yourself? You could buy and use a hard drive yourself, in the same way. Why invest in someone else's? Or for that matter, why should you have to go out and invest in one on your own? Would it not be better to just go out and *buy a normal book*, rather than invest in something that you do not really need? Do you really *need* to be trying to access something that is floating around in some mysterious "cloud," somewhere out there in cyberspace – and being charged money to do so? These new e-book marketing wizards seem to think so. It is amazing how far people will go to buy something that is far less from being a "thing" at all. More and more, every day, people are coming up with schemes to part you with your money and give you less and less in return.

The March of "Progress"

Another big problem with e-books is compatibility. In the mad rush to develop this new field of technology, multiple companies have created different formats that do not offer file support to their competitors. Therefore, many e-books are unusable on certain readers, forcing customers to buy and use the resident file format for that particular reader. Certain clouds do solve some compatibility problems, so that any e-reader can access the books, which is a good thing. This is the one potentially universal feature of a cloud that makes it viable for the future, and gives it some appeal. Another way around the compatibility issue is that with an e-reader you can use various conversion programs, some of which are free, to access your books. But it takes time to learn the programs and to execute the conversions – many of which are not clean or accurate, and litter the manuscript with mistakes that can sometimes make the entire book unreadable. Over time these problems will lesson, but all of this electronic hoop-jumping with its extra time and expense seems to complicate what you can get with a good old-fashioned book. Simple is always better. Keep It Simple, Stupid! The KISS rule – which is being ignored everywhere in today's world of technology, with a flood of gadgets that we do not really need being offered up like they hold some great earth-shattering importance, when in fact they are more of a *detriment* and a *distraction* than a blessing. But so much money is being put into the marketing of these items, that people will literally trample over each other in response to the hype, trying to get them, after standing in lines for hours upon the original release of some of them. These items are presented as having the ability to make our lives easier when, in fact, they complicate and confuse – and are more costly than something from the past that was quite basic in construction and simpler in design. Watch one of these home shopping network TV programs on any given day for a convincing view of the needless garbage being heaped upon the materialistic masses. Those who watch these shows and purchase these products are looking to feed their need to buy things more than being practical – truly practical – about their needs. It is this mindset that is being preyed upon by those selling the newest technology, and those who see it happening are those who tend to stick with real books.

It is no longer a quest to make things easier for us; it has become a quest to make money and to perfect the ability to convince the public that they need something which is, in most cases, totally unnecessary. Texting is a good example. A number of young people have been killed who were texting while driving, when they could have easily used a cell phone instead (this, also, is not recommended while driving, since it is illegal in most places – but it would have at least saved some lives if the victims chose to communicate with their voices). In 2012 a large wild bear had wandered into Los Angeles and was running through the streets. A TV news helicopter was covering the movements of the bear and showed a young man happily walking down an alley, _texting_. The bear came charging around the corner and into the alley while the young man continued to blindly walk and text, oblivious to the _wild bear_ that was racing straight towards him. Suddenly – and not a moment too soon – he noticed the bear, stopped texting and ran the other way. The point being, you don't have to be in a vehicle to put yourself in danger by texting. It requires intense focus, when you could instead be on the phone and be more aware of your surroundings. The moral of the story is, you never know when a wild bear will suddenly jump out at you. Remember this each time you start texting someone.

Many of the e-book formats that have flooded the market are also not needed. Most will disappear. They will become obsolete through constant upgrades in reading software, the replacement of operating formats, or the devices themselves will not survive due to financial failure, technical failure, or the popularity of their competitors. Here's an idea! You get none of this risk with a real book. You just buy the book. Period. Case closed. You have your information. Forget about upgrades or obsolete technology. Just open your book and read it.

I recently witnessed a young lady come into a bookstore who had just come from the beach. She said she was finished with her e-book reader and wanted to buy a real book. The battery for the device had gotten low at the beach and she was unable to charge it. So the device became unusable, and she was stuck without the ability to read. Not only that, before the battery died, it had slipped off the edge of her towel and sand had jammed the buttons and controls. She wasn't sure if it could ever be repaired and at that point she just didn't care. She was too frustrated to bother with it and switched back to normal books. As she was leaving with her purchase she also said that she liked the feel of holding a normal book in her hands anyway – and promised to return for more. It's a shame that too many are learning this only after their local bookstores have closed. If there is still a local bookstore near you that is open, please support it.

Real books are amazing, artistic and informative. It has taken us centuries to finally perfect them. Today, pages no longer turn yellow or get brittle due to the creation of acid free paper, so books will last even longer than many titles that have already survived for centuries. Due to advances in glue and adhesive surfaces, the bindings of paperbacks no longer crack and do not crease as easily. The ink is far better and doesn't fade or streak, and the printing press itself has been perfected to create amazing color and graphics. We have perfected the book and wouldn't you know it – as soon as that happens, some of us are ready to throw them aside in favor of electronic screens.

In reading a normal book, you will in most cases *see it* better – with less eyestrain, in consistent light and at a consistent size. Sure, you can blow up words on some reading devices, but then you lose continuity on most of them and can see only a few lines at a time, causing you to scroll incessantly. A certain "flow" is lost. You get more caught up in the mechanical action of scrolling than in reading the actual book. The larger pads and tablets have solved this problem to a degree, but then you lose the advantage of a more compact device that can fit in your pocket, which was always a big selling point for e-readers.

When you read normal sized text on a smaller reader, the resolution can be much less than with printed books, which results in eyestrain. Screen glare is also a common complaint. Using a normal book is often better on the eyes. If you must buy an e-reader, get a bigger tablet.

A book has two pliable "handles," meaning the front and back covers. It is easier to handle than most e-readers. You can also lend the book more easily if it's in physical form. Copying an e-book to someone else's device is always a hassle, but with a normal book, you just extend your hand with the book and give it to the interested recipient. It is truly a wonder to behold, as there is no technology involved. Just *friendship*. In such cases a nice bond or connection is formed. With e-readers, however, you are *separated* from others rather than being brought together. You are encouraged to isolate yourself with your personal little device – and this mindset, multiplied a million-fold, creates a society of socially defective people. Younger generations are being brought up with technology and gadgets in their hands, and a laser-like focus on these devices rather than other people. Some e-readers have the ability to allow you to "lend" your book to a friend for a limited time period – usually about two weeks. But what if something happens to delay them from finishing the book? It would be very annoying to be reading along and then have your screen go black, because your time ran out. With a real book, you just tell your friend that you're sorry and you'll return the book a few days later. Which usually works out fine. They don't rush over and grab the book out of your hands, declaring that your time is up, or demand that you go through an additional lending process or submit an application or an update to your status. Lending a book to someone should be easy. The only drawback with a real book is that you might never get it back. And that is because it is *real*. It actually exists, just like every other physical, tangible object. Lending books to people in this way is a great indicator of who you can actually trust in your life. If someone fails to return a book, you usually don't turn around and lend them another book or something more valuable – having learned a lesson about their character. Many people who have lost books this way are grateful because they turned down other requests from the same people to borrow lawn mowers, televisions, tools, dresses and make-up – and still have them today. With electronic devices we are privy to more volumes and bytes of information, including more e-books, but we learn less about each other because these devices act as a wedge between us all.

With information in general, it can be argued that modern devices now offer access to more helpful information than we have ever had in the past, which is good. But we are suffering from "information overload" as a result. We are missing the chance to work with these mountains of information in constructive ways because so much focus is being put on gathering it and accessing it, rather than *using* it. We've been trained to view things with blinders on and to not see a bigger, richer picture that is right there – available to us beyond the mere technological value. The extra few milliseconds in the speed of a device is being heralded as something far greater in importance than absorbing all the information in order to build a better world. Technological prowess supersedes reflective action.

We have become so dependent and lazy that we want *everything* served up to us on a silver platter just by pushing a button. Every single action or service that can be performed, on any level, that has not yet been invented to work instantly, with the push of a button, is being worked on by somebody. Inventors want to get rich and cater to the inherent laziness and stupidity that runs rampant in human society. If you can get it done by pushing a button with one finger, without thinking or moving very much, you will probably want to do it if your IQ is average or lower than average. On the other hand, you can choose to really *live your life* and be actively involved in it.

Instead of engaging in socially uplifting events or compassionate action on a local level, people would rather be entertained by sitting at home and pushing buttons. The level of gratification is easier to achieve and it takes less work to be gratified. Whether it be your TV, Internet, radio, microwave oven or e-book reader, everyone is rushing to push buttons while pushing everyone and everything else aside that should matter more to you, including loved ones.

Chapter Three

E-book Limitations

Large numbers of people who buy e-books are upset. There is protective software attached to many e-books called DRM, which stands for "Digital Rights Management." This prevents the user from copying and lending the book to others, like what is done with a normal book. With a physical book you are free to lend, give or resell it to others – as long as you do not copy it. It is copyrighted material, so you do not have the right to treat it like your own. Unlike with a physical book you need to copy an e-book first, before you can lend it. This violates the copyright. When you look at "first sale" rights, which is part of the law, it states that when you buy something you own it and can therefore do whatever you want with that one, single copy. You just can't "clone it" and go into business for yourself. That right belongs to the creator of the material. Nevertheless, all kinds of people are upset with e-book publishers for putting DRM on the files to prevent them from freely copying it.

First sale rights, however, apply to *physical objects*. You can lend, give or resell a physical object and once you have done this, *you don't have it anymore*. When you do it with a digital file, you still have the file and could therefore go into business for yourself, multiplying and providing it to others without end, which is what many people are doing (see next section below, under Piracy). People assume the final creation of a book file rests with the publisher, but digital files can be recreated by anyone – unless things like DRM are employed.

Because we are talking about digital files that are not tangible objects, consumers are not really buying these files or "books." They are only buying the right to access the digital file. They can harbor the file in some kind of *device* that they own – because the device is a physical object, so they own it. The only exception to this is a book file that is in the public domain, being an older work out of copyright that has already been legally designated as being owned by the public. That is the only exception.

For those who are claiming that e-books are really books, it must be made clear that this can never be the case. They are merely files and cannot be treated the same as real books, legally or in a physical way.

Because people have misconstrued what an e-book really is and what their rights are in relation to it, it has created negative feelings from the public toward e-book publishers who use DRM. This confusion and bitterness has led to widespread piracy, which is not good for books in any form.

Piracy

There was never anywhere near the level of book piracy going on in the past when you just had printed books. E-book technology has made it easy for people steal your book – and there are entire web sites devoted to this purpose – where you can go and download them for free, with virtually no repercussions for the perpetrators.

Publishers or authors can often go and view their own copyrighted material on these sites and find them available as free downloads. If you have a reasonably popular title check some of the torrent sites, and there's a good chance you will find your cherished work on there, pirated by thieves who openly give it away. These copyrighted e-books were stripped of their protective technology and put there, usually by some juvenile who never learned any respect for the hard work of others or developed scruples of any kind. On many occasions printed book versions (rather than e-books) are found that have been scanned and pirated, although thieves concentrate more on material that is already in e-book form. It's easier to steal.

These sites have a "wonderful" feature, however, made just for you! If you find your protected book on there and want to complain, they make it possible to report it to them, so they can "come to the rescue" and get it removed. Sometimes this is just a ruse, to make you think they are legitimately honest. But the very same people who have stolen your book have been known to run some of these sites. At the least, they are complicit because they enable these thefts daily, but appear ready to "help you" get it off. And for those who operate such sites and claim that they follow through and remove pirated works to the best of their ability, it may be true in some cases. They will do it to avoid trouble when they see it coming. Otherwise, they knowingly facilitate piracy – that is their purpose for being there, despite whatever claims they may make to the contrary. One company that seems legitimate and helpful is scribd.com because they have only a small percentage of pirated material that leaks in, and based on experience, they do their best to remove it. Many other sites, however, are devoted entirely to pirated material and should be avoided as a source for material.

With most of these companies you are required to fill out a lengthy form in the complaint process. You must include all the details of your pirated book – as if they didn't know this information already. They seem unconcerned that there is a copyright violation; they are more concerned to discover whether you, the complainer, is the true copyright holder. You must complete a separate form for every book, and are often asked to prove that you own the copyright when actually, anyone who posts a book should be required to be the copyright holder – and should therefore be the one to provide this proof before any posting should be allowed. It is a travesty when the real copyright holder is asked to prove ownership in the face of thousands of others who are, by default, allowed to claim this proof by being able to post the book. If you get through their claim form, a standard response is often experienced with bad news. You are informed that the book file is not really stored on their site, and that they merely contract with the original site that has your book and they access it by getting a feed of some kind from this other storage site. You are told that their "hands are tied." They provide you with information on how to contact this mysterious, hidden site – and when you try to contact them you do in fact discover that it is hidden and you often cannot get to it in any effective way. These sites are often based in foreign countries or "offshore locations" that allow them to hide your files and their entire presence. E-books really are a great innovation. For pirates.

Sometimes a torrent site will get your book removed – a seemingly wonderful but often empty gesture. Because as soon as the book goes down, another pirate (or the same one who loaded it the first time) comes along and loads it again within a matter of days – or hours – to replace it, and you must start the process all over again. Sometimes, the person who uploads the book back on to the site is the very person who was so "very kind" and took it off for you. Or any one of thousands of other people who upload pirated books or movies to these sites could notice that all of a sudden your prized work was no longer there, and would immediately upload it. You will often find multiple copies of the same book or film on these sites, which were uploaded from numerous sources, depending on popularity. Most of these sites have chat rooms or bulletin boards where requests are constantly made – and there's always someone out there willing to track down and post requested items just to see if they can find it.

To date, only the largest of these sites have been shut down. When this happens, some have been known to boldly announce on their old home page that they are moving to an offshore haven where they can operate with impunity. Well-known "safe havens" exist for when it gets too hot. Then they change their names, announce their move and keep right on going with business as usual. All their customers jump over with them.

As of this writing there is legislation pending that would allow the U.S. government to "seize" the actual URLs or registered web addresses of those engaged in piracy, and to issue orders to all servers and other sites having any connection whatsoever to them to not engage in business with them or assist them in any way, or they would be prosecuted for aiding and abetting these operations. So someone is listening. The problem, however, is that such legislation is being fought by those who are using the constitutional right of "free speech" as a shield, so it is yet to be seen as to when or if this type of legislation will be passed. Sometime in the near future some form of this legislation may be passed. If it does, true rights holders will begin to get at least some relief from this currently out of control activity. Estimates show that 20% of all e-books have been pirated, and the number is growing.

Only the author or publisher of a book should be allowed to post it for free or give permission to do so (unless it is in the public domain). Since many others besides the rights holders are doing it, and proliferating the Internet with all kinds of free material, people are forming the opinion that they should not have to pay for anything if it happens to be on the Net. For example, people have paid for their physical magazine and newspaper subscriptions for years. But as soon as you put a newspaper on the Internet by paid subscription, people will often refuse it. For some reason, they feel entitled to get it for free, if it's digital. When the *Times* of London began asking for a $4 per week subscription fee, they lost 90% of their online readership. When the same information does not appear in a solid physical form, people automatically devalue it. Many papers have folded because of this, or drastically cut back their staffs or expenses in order to stay solvent.

A sarcastic article recently appeared in a publishing newsletter about money. It proposed that the writer should be allowed to copy off money and just use it as he saw fit, employing the same idiotic logic used by thousands of Internet proponents for "free information." It's absurd to think anyone could pirate money, but protected intellectual property is no different. Only the government has the right to print money, and only authors have the right to print their books or designate a publisher to do so. Authors and publishers need to be afforded the same respect as governments who print money. The only difference is it takes just a few minutes for a government printing press to run off legal tender, while it may take years for an author to research and write his book.

Authors are becoming more prevalent these days. A movement has sprung up to push legitimate publishers aside. New technology allows people to self publish when many had previously failed to enlist the help and commitment of a true publisher – which was no small feat. Literally millions of people are rushing into the publishing business with their own (often substandard) material. Many are not only ignorant writers, but know nothing of publishing law – making the mistaken assumption that they can take and publish other people's protected literary property in addition to their own.

The Coming Age of Ignorance

There are Internet arguments put forth by people who are convinced that all information should be free – despite the fact that some books are painstakingly researched for up to twenty years, in some cases, and then protected, with the hope of making an income from it. Writing a book is just like any other job, but the worker is usually paid later for his efforts – unless he is one of the lucky few to get a publisher's advance. Being a writer is enough of a struggle without the added disrespect and thievery by pirates. Writers, just like everyone else, do not like to work for free. It's a profession. There should be a study done as to why people think information should be free. No one believed this in the past. Now that news is free in many places, it seems many people are mistaking news for legitimate research and copyright protected material. There are different types of information; it is not all the same and should not be treated the same.

It may also have something to do with information moving more quickly today and becoming more accessible through all the electronic gadgets we now have. It is primarily young people doing the pirating, so perhaps the younger generation has never been instilled with enough moral fiber to respect the intellectual property of others, or maybe it is a way to get back at publishers who rejected their work. Or perhaps, the material these people steal and distribute has more merit and interest than what they could do themselves, so the pirate gains attention by providing something he would otherwise not be able to. Offering something of *value* for free brings you attention. The *value* a pirate receives is not monetary, but comes in the form of a boost to his self-esteem.

As opposed to pirates, those who innocently believe information should be free and disseminate it could be getting news mixed up with literature, research or copyright protected non-fiction material. News is free on the Internet almost everywhere and this has put a big dent in newspapers. Once news has been received and read once, its value is at its peak. In general, it is of little value beyond the day it is transmitted. However books are not news. The daily news is good for one day – books, however, are timeless. Many young people do not even read books. Their attention spans are too short, having been geared to tweets on twitter, emails and other brief snippets that the pace of society demands. Those who fail to enrich themselves with the deeper knowledge of books only contribute to the level of ignorance we experience today that we did not have in the past – for example, like the piracy of intellectual property. These types of thefts always did occur in the past – but nowhere near the extent that we are experiencing today.

Much of this thievery is made possible by the avalanche of gadgets, gizmos and other computerized technology that permeates our culture, which in turn enables a new breed of pirate that can steal things more easily. They can hide behind firewalls, offshore accounts, and can get away with electronic thievery more safely than by making a physical appearance to rob you. Internet thievery and scams of various kinds are running rampant.

Society is showing signs of a meltdown because one powerfully rotten segment is thwarting the creative and artistic expression of another, making it difficult for the creative group to continue to make a living. Who is going to continue writing great works if they know some loser hidden away in his parent's basement, unable to create something like this for himself, is going to pirate it off and send it all over the Internet for free? This destroys a great deal of income that was worked very hard for – but can be lost in minutes due to the callous actions of a stranger. Multiply this outcast in the basement (bereft of social skills in the first place, due to a warped life with computers), by the few thousand people engaged in this same activity and you essentially pull the plug on the motivation and creativity of many truly gifted people. Doing this sort of thing (putting truly talented writers and other artists out of business) is a way to "make room" for all of the mediocre material being self-published and pumped through many of the same channels, whether it be music, literature or any other creatively induced product. Piracy really does hurt our most creative storytellers who might, over the next few decades, become lost in the coming avalanche of mediocrity and be much harder to find. Little incentive will be left for them to produce material unless something is done to protect their creative work from free Internet distribution and other forms of piracy.

It might be argued that great talent will always emerge and be recognized, which is true. But piracy shortens the careers of talented people who depend on proper income from their work, and would otherwise give up if the required income fails. If piracy continues at the rate we find today, we will all lose access to future creations that will never be made. The mediocre will dominate. Virtually all of the personal electronic gadgets out there support this activity and create an easier means to share pirated material. E-books are a big part of this, due to the ease of file transfer, converting the files or using other gadgets to scan the original pages. If you are reading this book on a computer or device of any kind, it is pirated and it is requested that you respect and support those involved in its creation by purchasing the paper version and deleting the electronic one.

All told, trying to prevent piracy in this day and age is virtually impossible. If publishers spent their time trying to protect their work, they would never have the time to get any new books published or would go broke paying someone to fight it, because of the non-stop hours involved that will send you into a continuous, frustrating loop. This rampant thievery takes place in an electronic world that did not exist anywhere near this level with normal printed books. An online infringement detection service called iCopyright does exist, but it's unclear to this writer how affordable or effective it really is. Most publishers just shrug and hope the extra exposure from piracy may inspire a few honest people to purchase a real *printed version* of their book as a consolation.

With a digital e-book, the chances of your book being pirated increases about a hundredfold. Many publishers have been reluctant to publish their books digitally for this very reason – however it is reaching the point where publishers are being *forced* to do so. The income being lost from printed books is going into the e-book market, so if a publisher wants to remain solvent, the company must produce digital versions to make up that loss. However, piracy cuts into the potential to make up these losses during such a crucial, transitional time for publishers. Publishers will continue to be needed. They will maintain relationships with the best writers and continue to preserve, build and market the better-written material to the public.

What these pirates don't understand is how badly they affect the already damaged economy with their actions. There will always be unconscious, self-serving idiots out there who do these sorts of things, but it has never occurred on this level before – mainly because e-book formats make it so incredibly easy. The DRM security format is extremely easy to strip from a file, and the instructions and software needed to do so may be easily found on the Internet by anyone who wants it. The publishing industry is in crisis. Those forces working to topple it are advocating the elimination of DRM protection (to them, a nuisance requiring extra steps) while stealing whatever they want through electronic technology.

Jobs are harder to find for the youth of America and this should be a concern. You have countries like China, which has a strong economy through hard-working industrious people, competing with the youth of America. Many owners of big businesses have sent their companies overseas, often to China, to exploit cheap labor and this has robbed the American youth of many jobs. A number of companies have realized this mistake and are actually bringing their companies back home to America. But in the meantime, many younger Americans have lost their work ethic. They have been "dumbed down" by diminished educational standards, so have taken less challenging jobs or resort to taking unethical shortcuts to whatever success they can achieve. This damages the US economy even more.

Ethics and other courses rooted in philosophy are not taught in schools except in some colleges on a limited basis. Young people in America and other countries are not trained to think. This lack of thought encourages people to read less – and those who continue to read want to do it quickly, with less depth, so opt for e-books. Therefore, it is not only the printed book that is dying – it is the very fabric of our thinking and our ability to do it on a meaningful level.

E-books are good for quick information, but few people like to spend hours staring at a screen because eyestrain and computer vision syndrome (CVS) can result. With older monitors, screens would refresh slowly so we would see flickering. Today LCD screens are said to refresh a hair faster than the eye's perception. It is my contention, however, that the brain, although not conscious of it, is constantly readjusting and interpreting varying pixelated levels that can cause eyestrain. True or not, people tire faster and read for shorter durations when using screens rather than a normal book. Take a random poll. Most will prefer a regular book – unless they have been brought up to never open one, which makes them part of the "dumbing down" process.

Privacy Concerns and Violations

If the readers of e-books are being dumbed down, who is getting smarter? The software connected to e-books and their sites can track you. You would be surprised what can be known about you. This software can tell whoever is monitoring it many things about your usage – the times you are on the computer, how many pages you viewed, what times you had accessed the information, exactly what you are reading, and how often you read it. Why do they want to know this? Demographic information is important to many companies. What you think, do and buy can be determined quite easily. They want to know how to target you for additional sales, or share your information (for a price) with other companies or agencies that want to know more about you. In the age of the Internet and advanced technology, a great deal of privacy, whether you know it or not, is lost just by purchasing an e-book. Those who would want to keep these hidden intrusions out of their lives should stick to traditional books.

Companies keep track of you in very elaborate ways, so that even without tracking the books you read directly, they can still get a good idea of what you might be reading based on Facebook, your amazon.com and Google searches, and even through your purchases at the supermarket, should you have a card that gets scanned when you check out. Your profile exists in the databases of many large companies and you do not even know about. Therefore, you have no control over what they do with your data. Virtually everything you buy using anything electronic creates some sort of record for the benefit of others. Avid book buyers, whether it be e-book or printed ones, can attribute this invasion of privacy to online purchases, search activity or by simply browsing or surfing the Net. Those who prefer to keep their lives as private as possible do in fact buy real printed books, and only from a local, independent bookstore (rather than a chain) in order to avoid this. Yes, such people really do exist because they value their privacy more than others. I have met a number them. They prefer to keep their information as private as possible – not because they are criminals and hiding, but because their information is supposed to be private unless *they* make the decision to share it.

The sad fact is that Americans and many people around the world no longer have control over their private information. Those days are gone. Many people consider the gathering and sharing of private information to be a blatant intrusion. Some may argue that you have, in fact, given permission to share your information because the "agreement" you made is in the small print of various services and credit card companies that you may be involved with. However, there is a certain degree of duress involved along with the deceptive fine print. Unless you agree to this you are denied the ability to use their services, which, in many cases, you need to function as a normal member of society.

One final and important note on privacy and your e-book reader. Through a standard e-book reader, your purchases and reading choices can be tracked. But most e-book readers are multi-functional. Its single-purpose feature is predicted to be completely gone in a few years. With units becoming more "useful" and widespread, bigger concerns are emerging due to the use in most of them of a hidden application called

Carrier IQ. Few people have heard of it, but CIQ software does not require the knowledge or consent of the user in order to operate in their device. It is extremely difficult or impossible to disable. According to David Rosen from AlterNet, in his article "Are You Being Tracked?" (www.alternet.org/story/153592/are_you_being_tracked_8_ways_your_privacy_is_being_eroded_online_and_off), Carrier IQ is currently installed on about "150 million wireless devices offered through AT&T, HTC, Nokia, RIM (Blackberry), Samsung, Sprint and Verizon Wireless. It runs on a number of operating systems, including the Apple OS and Google's Android (but not on Microsoft Windows)." This includes your e-book reader if it is multi-functional and falls into the above-mentioned categories. In addition to Carrier IQ, there could be other hidden programs coming, or already in your device that you are completely unaware of.

On Android phones, CIQ can store your text messages, record phone calls, track a user's keystrokes, and pinpoint your exact location. Yes, that's right, it seems the recipient can know where you are at all times, if your device is on, what you've been saying, who you've been saying it to, and basically everything that you've been doing. Tracking keystrokes is one of the most negative, intrusive activities of *spyware* and people will do anything to get rid of it if found on their computers. But you are supposed to passively accept it in exchange for using the newest, nifty device that might contain it. If you happen to own an Android phone, would you have voluntarily agreed to this at the time of your purchase?

The Carrier IQ company, backed by a group of "venture capitalists," according to Rosen, was founded in 2005 and is located in Mountain View, California. CIQ's VP of Marketing, Andrew Coward, reportedly told the Associated Press that the FBI has contacted them for data, but the FBI has failed to issue a "clarification" as to what the data was being used for. This lack of clarity points one's thoughts toward the illegal wiretapping of phone systems throughout America during G. W. Bush's administration in an eerily reminiscent way, and could easily represent the next level of advanced and illegal snooping upon the American public (and upon others, throughout the world). Clearly, this hidden little program is the closest thing to "big brother" we have ever had. A savvy researcher might be inspired to learn more about who these backing "venture capitalists" of CIQ really are, what their backgrounds are, who their business contacts have been, and what *they* have been up to. The public has a right to be suspicious of these people, based on the reportedly hidden nature of their software. Sure, it's possible there may not have been any hidden agenda regarding their software at all. They could have been out to make a buck at your expense only – but possible FBI intrusion into your data makes one wonder. It's not likely they would have tested this app on themselves first, gathered all the sensitive data on what *they* were doing, and saved the information for future use. Just like us, they would of course consider such data to be *none of our business.*

Now that people are finally becoming aware of this app, questions are being raised. Nevertheless, you cannot go in and have this program removed. It is virtually intrinsic to the device it is connected to. The only reason CIQ was exposed is because a security researcher from a potentially rival company blew the whistle on them – otherwise we would all still be in the dark. What else don't we know about? And if and when the plug gets pulled on CIQ, who's to know if another rival company, waiting in the wings, will take its place and be even more intrusive (and more hidden) than Carrier IQ?

To be fair to Carrier IQ, Rosen states in his article, "According to the company, its software is designed to improve mobile communications. CIQ is used to help businesses with GPS tracking of mobile devices and coordinate employee travel. The company initially denied there was anything suspicious about its software. Further analysis revealed a bug that allowed SMS messages to be captured.... In the wake of the mounting scandal, most of the nation's leading wireless providers are modifying how they implement CIQ."

I've never heard of a "bug" that accidentally finds and captures messages. In his article, Rosen also identified other companies being challenged for alleged intrusion and tracking. My advice? Don't trust e-book readers, multi-functional or not, if you are concerned with personal information being gathered intrusively. Buy a normal book and a phone from a trusted company, turn your ringer off for a while, sit back with a cool drink, and enjoy your book in a personal way, without anyone "reading over your shoulder." Which, by the way, is a very uncomfortable feeling. Turn some real pages and relax. Why on earth do people invite so many intrusions into their lives?

Independent Book Stores

In the past ten years, record numbers of independent bookstores have been forced to close their doors. The Internet has made it more convenient for people to buy books, should they know what they are looking for, so independent stores have suffered. The big chains have also played a role, but now, even the Borders bookstore chain has fallen victim to the Internet and closed all of their stores across the country in the middle of 2011. And now, e-books have come along and started nipping at the heels of the independent stores and publishing companies that favor paper. With e-books it has now become possible to publish books without using any paper whatsoever. Entire companies have sprung up that publish only e-books and have never once published a paper book. The real reason some new publishers avoid using paper is because it's easier. They never have to touch anything except a keyboard. They use the excuse of how going paperless "saves the environment." However, e-readers are notorious for containing a variety of toxic materials that pose more danger to the environment than paper does (paper can be recycled while toxic materials must be disposed of properly). See below, under Environmental Concerns, for more.

Many nonsensical factors conspire against the good old-fashioned independent bookstore. For example, let me tell you about my neighborhood. In San Diego, for many years Adams Avenue in Normal Heights was known as "book row," and had a legendary reputation. In 2001 there were at least 12 different stores within a few blocks along the avenue. It was a utopia for books. People would drive from as far away as Los Angeles to stay the weekend and browse through them all for their entire stay. Today, in 2012, there are only two of these stores left – the large and impressive Adams Avenue Bookstore (highly recommended) and The Book Tree. Some people have come into The Book Tree and begged them to never close, saying how important the store is to them. No promises can be made; such stores will remain open only as long as they are able.

The world's most famous metaphysical bookstore, the legendary Bodhi Tree, once located in Los Angeles, was patronized for decades by some of Hollywood's most interesting celebrities in addition to the general public. However, they have recently closed. This kind of thing has been happening all over the country, to the disappointment of book people everywhere. A small fraction of independent stores remain, and it is feared that one day, just like with music stores, they will be virtually gone. Most people download their music from the Internet. A large portion of it is *pirated*, causing a great deal of outcry and complaints, so artists get even less revenue than they would have when people would buy their CDs or vinyl in stores. It is a shame what technology has done to the ability of creative artists to make a living, whether they be authors of music or books. They put their lives and passion into their work, and make far less money due to rampant worldwide, electronic piracy that seems to be spreading.

The publishing of paper books and the existence of bookstores support authors through their royalties and book sales. Less income is made from digital sales (unless the author sells directly), due to their lesser price, in a world where the average professional writer makes only $5000 per year from sales of standard books. Support your local bookstores, whether they are independents or chains. Support them. You don't want to see books found only in museums one day – unless you are an investor in digital media with ruthless and greedy intentions.

The Advantage of Paper

Physical books have many redeeming qualities that would be otherwise lost. A book is a solid, physical object that can be held in your hand, rather than being hidden away in some kind of device. It therefore has a look and "personality" all its own. The cover has artwork that is well thought out and meant to be appreciated as an artistic creation. It is displayed more clearly and easily than the e-book rendition found only on one "page," hidden in a reading device. The resolution of a physical book cover is not compromised like the "cover" of an e-book, due to a transfer into pixels onto a screen that often has lower visual quality than you would otherwise experience. With a real book you can appreciate the color and meaning of the cover more fully – and don't have to scroll in order to see it all.

With a standard book you can feel every page as you turn them and are more involved in the reading experience with the tactile sensations of the book in your hands. You are directly engaged with the book rather than having it interpreted for you by an artificial device that has been manufactured for the sole purpose of offering you a "counterfeit" version. Pushing buttons and looking at a screen will never come close to reading a genuine book.

Your eyes will not be as strained with a genuine book. As previously mentioned, I believe the light emitted from a reading device bombards the eyes with streams of varying light levels at an extremely fast rate – so fast that you are not conscious of the immense fluctuations that the eyes and brain must decipher. This would literally freak out your brain as it attempts to sort out these hypersensitive computerized signals. A real book in steady light cannot do this.

We retain more information when we read from printed books rather than from computer screens. In a study conducted by Jacob Nielsen, it was found that people read, on average, 25% faster from printed materials than from computerized screens. (http://en.wikipedia. org/wiki/Screen_reading)

Computers are good for finding articles or interesting facts in support of research (see last paragraph), but due to the time involved, I would never desire to read an entire book this way. For example, Nicholas Carr wrote an article for Wired Magazine in 2010 called "The Web Shatters Focus, Rewires Brains," showing the effects of computerized reading and how it scrambles and rewires the brain. As of this writing, it can be found at http://www.wired.com/magazine/2010/05/.

Many e-books are meant to be read online. To find them, people are often sent to their locations through what is called hyperlinks. Some publishers think that hyperlinks (words highlighted, usually in blue, that allow you to jump to other articles that detail more information about that subject) make an e-book more fancy and desirable. The industry is currently promoting the "perfect e-book" as being stuffed with various hyperlinks for "additional information" purposes – but are also used for clever sales pitches whenever people can get away with it.

The following paragraph is quoted from the above-mentioned article by Carr.

> Research continues to show that people who read linear text comprehend more, remember more, and learn more than those who read text peppered with links. In a 2001 study, two scholars in Canada asked 70 people to read *The Demon Lover*, a short story by Elizabeth Bowen. One group read it in a traditional linear-text format; they'd read a passage and click the word *next* to move ahead. A second group read a version in which they had to click on highlighted words in the text to move ahead. It took the hypertext readers longer to read the document, and they were seven times more likely to say they found it confusing.

Other tests show that when links increase, comprehension decreases. And you do not have to click on the links at all. Just by being there, they diminish your comprehension of the material. Their very presence is a proven distraction to the brain and it must figure out in every case, whether consciously or unconsciously, if you should click on it or not. And this is the "exciting new direction" that e-books are going in – crammed with "interesting" links. So if you want to scramble your brain and follow their cue, be my guest.

A number of hypertext experiments in 2007 found the same results – that jumping between digital documents robs your comprehension and understanding of what you are trying to read. Additional research also suggests that when you add other types of links to surround these hyperlinks, like advertisements, videos, sidebars or images of any other sort, comprehension is diminished even more.

We should not be rushing to insert hyperlinks into e-books based on the studies being done and books like *The Shallows: What the Internet Is Doing to Our Brains*, by Nicholas Carr. In 2005, two psychologists with the Centre for Applied Cognitive Research at Carleton University in Canada reviewed a collection of *38 different experiments*, all of which involved the reading of hyperlinked content. The psychologists, DiStefano and LeFevre, found no support for the initial theory that hyperlinks create better comprehension, but instead showed that the increased demand of hyperlinked text impaired reading performance and stymied comprehension.

In a paper published in *The Journal of Research in Reading*, Norwegian researcher Ann Mangen attributes the loss of retention to the actions a reader must take to do their reading. These actions occur at a distance from the text itself – text which is located inside the computer, e-book or mobile phone. These actions include clicking a mouse, scrolling with keys, or pointing or scrolling with touch pads. She states, "Materiality matters… One main effect of the intangibility of the digital text is that of making us read in a shallower, less focused way."

You lose the feeling of being in touch with your text, and the extra work needed to "grasp" it, scatters you.

People say that having the book in their hands "feels good." It feels even better while reading it because you are in touch with the information more. And there are differences. The cover is thicker than the rest of the book, so you have variation in the object rather than one unchangeable mass that requires only automated functions to operate.

Everything looks and feels the same with a reading device, so the process loses some tactile sensation and becomes more automated and mechanical.

A true book lover goes to bookstores and appreciates the look and feel of physical books while they browse. And they also appreciate the smell. Some people can almost get high from opening an old book, putting their nose into the middle of it and smelling deeply. With the right book the smell can be euphoric (okay, I admit it, I'm hooked). A reading device has no smell unless you stick it under your arm for a while – which I would not recommend. This is something I am *not* hooked on, and prefer the paper alternative.

With a physical book, all of the senses come into play except for sound. An e-book can use sound in ways a normal book cannot. But quiet is *good* for reading. That's why we have libraries. You must be quiet when you read in libraries because noise is a *distraction* and a nuisance. I would not prefer my e-book reader to double as a phone, or have a bunch of other little chimes or audio indicators going off when I'm trying to read. By trying to make modern devices more "important," we've only made them more annoying.

Some e-books can actually read themselves to you, as well as books on CD. You just sit and passively listen, like you would if at a lecture. This is good when you are driving a vehicle, or if you are blind, or have poor eyesight; but otherwise it can be irritating. Often times people will buy a book on tape or have a computer read them a book, only to discover shortly thereafter that they cannot stand the voice that is reading it. If this is the case and you really want the information, you could be stuck in an uncomfortable situation, like being forced to listen to fingernails scraping on a blackboard. *Engage your mind.* Pick up a normal book and read it for yourself – unless you truly need audio for the above-mentioned reasons. You're not a child anymore so if you're still looking for someone to read to you, it may be time to grow up and start doing these things for yourself. Barring poor eyesight or listening while you drive, the general rule should be if you feed yourself, you should read for yourself.

Studying and problem solving, found commonly in academics, are other areas to consider normal books for, as primary sources of information. Schools are turning toward gadgets due to their convenience, but retaining the information is more important than convenience. Occam's Razor, as mentioned in Chapter One, is a general law that philosophers often adhere to when attempting to solve a problem. It requires that one choose the easiest, least complex answer to a problem because the answer that makes the most sense is usually the correct one. In the quest for researching important information from either a book or e-book, a philosopher would likely choose a physical book. They have been around for centuries and are simpler and more trusted. You will not encounter corruption issues, crashes, data loss or a host of other unforeseen problems with a normal, everyday book.

If, however, a trained philosopher requires large amounts of data to search for limited information, he will choose the use of a computer. It saves time and the chances for electronic problems diminish with limited use. If only a few good sources must be studied closely, however, then the best choice is the physical book. Reasons, as outlined in *this* book, include information retention, less eyestrain, fewer distractions and, for some, privacy issues – making it clear that intelligence should not always gravitate, automatically, to technology.

Environmental Concerns

One of the most popular arguments in favor of e-books is that they can displace paper, protect the environment and prevent the depletion of trees. Trees help create the oxygen that all life needs to survive. We have cut down too many and need to stop their depletion. Trees need to be replaced and much work is being done in this direction. To take the burden off the demand, a great deal of paper is recycled. If any paper product should fail to reach a recycling center, however, it is in large part biodegradable (meaning it will break down and be naturally absorbed into the earth).

It would seem that e-book devices are better because there is no paper involved. But we need to look into this further. E-book readers are made out of plastic, Rare Earth Elements (REEs), various circuits and batteries. Therefore, unlike paper, they are non-biodegradable. Various toxic substances are required to produce them, and the disposal of their batteries is an environmental concern. Very few companies are forthcoming about exactly what their devices contain. But they are quick to tell us what their devices do *not* contain when a certain toxic substance is missing, but we will never know about the other toxic ingredients it does have. This should be a concern.

Technology changes so rapidly that people often joke about how your device is obsolete by the time you get it home from the store. It is not quite that bad, but the turnover rate and subsequent trashing of these devices can inject large amounts of toxic waste into the environment that do not biodegrade as easily as paper. Paper products are more sustainable and reusable, and do not require the Rare Earth Elements found in electronic devices.

Rare Earth Elements are a collection of 17 chemical elements that appear in the periodic table together and are all metals. Four of them in particular – terbium, gadolinium, lutetium and dysprosium – are used in the manufacture of iPads, e-readers, cell phones, laptops, medical devices, LCD TVs and other electronic devices, but are in short supply. A recent discovery of deposits at the bottom of the Pacific Ocean created some excitement but will still not break a Chinese monopoly on its supply for at least another ten years, according to a Popular Mechanics article called "Why Deep-Sea Rare-Earth Metals Will Stay Where They Are – For Now," by Rob Goodier, from July 8, 2011. China controls about 97% of the world's supply of REEs and has begun to cut exports to supply domestic consumption, causing prices to rise. This trend is expected to continue for as long as they control the market. In October 2011, China announced they were closing some of their rare-earth processing plants due to environmental concerns. It is common knowledge that many rare-earth mines in China have been operating with no regulations, causing severe environmental hazards due to the profits that can be made. How many faulty plants are still in operation is a big question.

Previous finds in the United States were abandoned because the elements are too difficult and costly to extract in environmentally safe ways. For example, there were a number of major radioactive wastewater spills in protected lands in the Mojave Desert in the late 1990's – so we abandoned REE mining and left it to China, a country that has had less concern in the past with similar issues. They have also had a habit of sending unsafe items laced with dangerous chemicals to consumers the world over. But due to China's REE cutbacks, two plants in other countries are newly opened – one in Australia (which China had previously tried to invest in and control) and one in the U.S. in Mountain Pass, California.

How toxic and how dangerous is the mining of REEs? Far more than with the creation of paper. The remaining information in this paragraph is paraphrased or quoted from an article called "China's Rare Earth Elements Industry: What Can The West Learn?, by Cindy Hurst, which can be found on docs.google.com. Most of the REE mining in China is done in what is called the Baotou region. Statistics gathered from this region report that "all the rare earth enterprises in the Baotou region produce approximately ten million tons of all varieties of waste water every year" and most of it is "discharged without being effectively treated, which not only contaminates potable water for daily living, but also contaminates the surrounding water environment and irrigated farmlands." This is similar to what happened in the Mojave Desert and caused the U.S. to abandon their original project. All of the fish died in the Yellow River in the Baotou since they dump a variety of radioactive chemicals into it – a river that 150 million people in China depend on for their primary source of water. A number of people in their 30s have died from working around the mines, as many refuse to wear their masks due to the oppressive heat. The article by Hurst exposes far more; this is only the tip of the iceberg. The main point being made is that mining Rare Earth Elements for things like your e-reader and other devices is contributing to some extremely nasty, rotten and toxic conditions that are not even remotely similar to producing paper. Paper mills once used chemicals and polluted their waterways, but have since eliminated most of the worst chemicals through scientific research – thereby diminishing pollution levels in many plants worldwide.

Recycling

Very little has been done to recycle Rare Earth Elements. Programs have started in a few countries, but remain inefficient on a number of levels due to the costs involved. These devices are made to be discarded, not recycled, and it is less costly to throw them away than recycle them. Just looking at them makes it clear – you must pry these devices apart to get to the various components to recycle, which are small and very time-consuming to extract. In general, third-world countries are used to recycle REEs because they are able to hire the low-pay workers needed to make these facilities profitable.

The vast majority of all electronic devices are thrown into landfills. This has been the case for many years and will remain this way for many years to come. No one will repair their devices when they break because the units are almost always outdated when they reach this point, and the labor to repair them is at least as much as buying a new one. So landfills will continue to fill up with devices, including e-readers that contain toxic materials. Most landfills do not have protective liners or fully adequate systems to catch these toxic materials as they slowly leach out into the surrounding ground water and communities.

Overseas recycling centers have the same problem. In many developing countries, funds are not available to take proper precautions. Unprotected workers are paid almost nothing while they attempt to pry anything of value out of this equipment. They are exposed all day to toxicity, while piles of equipment are left outdoors to leach toxins into the ground and surrounding communities.

Although companies like Apple and Amazon have recycling programs in place, there is still a long way to go to make them more effective. They should be applauded for being there, but consumers in general do not like to recycle their electronic devices when it is easier to sneak them into the trash and be done with it. Over 80 per cent of this material ends up in U. S. landfills because of apathy, ignorance or laziness.

Recycling programs must improve to the point where people will respond properly. More importantly, these programs the world over must also act responsibly and dispose of this waste safely. According to the Electronic Takeback Coalition, most recycling companies do not recycle locally at all, but export their electronics to overseas companies because it is less costly. Apple is an exception, having claimed that all of their e-waste is processed in the U.S. and not shipped overseas (http://www.apple.com/hotnews/agreenerapple/). Many of these foreign companies, located mostly in Asia and Africa, dismantle the devices under unsafe conditions. This endangers people's health – whether it be the workers directly, or through contamination of the surrounding land, water tables and air. Anywhere from 50 to 80 per cent of all e-waste collected in the U.S. is shipped overseas for recycling.

The failure of recycling programs should not be as big a worry as electronic waste going directly into landfills or being incinerated. The most recent numbers available come from 2007. According to the EPA, three million tons of electronic waste was generated by Americans in 2007, while only 13.6 per cent of it was recycled. This means the remaining 86.4 per cent of it went into our landfills (where the toxic chemicals can potentially leach into our water supplies), or incinerated, causing these chemicals to be spewed into the air. Since 2007 the tonnage of electronic waste has undoubtedly increased, which makes matters only worse, and might explain why data is lacking since then. Tablets are currently predicted to replace e-readers completely at some future point, due to their versatility, so you can expect millions of e-readers to one day end up in local landfills.

Many of the largest makers of e-readers remain less than forthcoming about the chemicals present in their e-reading devices because no one wants to raise concern or sabotage their own business. Apple is the only company that provides environmental data on its products and is at least showing some concern. Casey Harrell of Greenpeace, which monitors the environmental impact of consumer electronics, told the *New York Times*, "I don't know what chemicals are in or out," in reference to various e-book devices. The focus of these companies, in this regard, seems to be more on profits than safety – to tell you only when a certain chemical is *not* present, and exclude mention of the dangerous ones that might remain. At least with paper, you know exactly what you are dealing with.

Every time you turn on an e-reading device you are using power. Not so with a book – you just open it and use your own power (mind power) to read it. There are no buttons, bells, pop-ups, links, low batteries or other distractions to annoy you.

The ecological footprint of a book is less than an e-book reader. The industry always compares books to e-book files – not books to the reading devices themselves, where the attention should be going. Some believe that saving paper by using an electronic device is "the answer" of the future. However, books – especially from a school library – can be used and shared by multiple students over the years, which saves many copies from being produced. E-readers are individual devices, made more for profit by the manufacturer since *everyone* who wants access to a book must have the device first. Only then can they get the e-book – which also must be used on an individual basis. The point is that e-reading devices have been produced by the millions and clearly cause more environmental damage than paper books do.

A forest is a natural, renewable and biodegradeable resource. Plastics, circuits and toxic chemicals are not.

You need to constantly charge your e-reader until one day your battery will die. Can you recall the last time you had to plug in a paper book and wait around before you could read it? Is there any additional extension to a book that you periodically must replace just for the privilege of being able to continue reading it?

If you drop an e-reader and it breaks or comes apart, make sure your child does not put any pieces in his or her mouth, as small children are apt to do. These broken parts could be extremely toxic. Loose pieces could masquerade as candy, and you might have to call poison control.

If your child happens to ingest a piece of paper, this is much less of a concern – you will never have to pump his stomach.

After a book is made, that is end of its strain on the system. Its carbon footprint is done. Sure, it takes plenty of water and the use of some chemicals by paper mills to produce books, so it still takes its toll. But with an e-reader or other related gadget, their impact on the environment will continue for years to come.

Are Paper Books Really That Bad?

There are those who will argue that the use of paper for books has become so bad that it is a bigger environmental concern than what electronic devices are composed of. The rainforests, they say, are disappearing at an alarming rate and we need these trees to allow the planet to "breath," and create oxygen for us and everything else on the planet. However, what they do not understand is that the stripping of the rainforests is directly related to cattle farming and wood products, and not the paper industry. For example, according to wikipedia (http://en.wikipedia.org/wiki/Deforestation_in_Brazil), the Brazilian government initially attributed 38% of all forest loss between 1966 and 1975 to large-scale cattle ranching. And according to the Guardian (http://www.guardian.co.uk/commentisfree/cifamerica/2011/jun/12/brazil-amazon-rainforest), deforestation in the Brazilian rainforests rose 27% from August 2010 to April 2011, largely due to soybean plantations. Most of the harvested soybeans go to China to feed the cattle they raise for beef. Finding any statistics on paper manufacturing from rainforests is virtually impossible because so little of it is done.

Rainforest trees are mostly used for timber, rubber, wood chips, cardboard and firewood or are wasted in the "slash and burn" process. Often, before a burn, the most valuable trees are removed. Villagers and large steel plants are also known to burn trees to create charcoal.

Paper books still use trees from other areas, however. With this in mind, we will compare which is greener, paper books or e-readers.

E-readers are supposed to save trees by eliminating paper – but what saves far more trees is a vegetarian. Using an e-reader doesn't even come close. It is widely reported that each and every vegetarian saves about one acre of trees every year. One average, paper-producing tree puts out about 20 reams of paper (500 twenty lb. sheets of 8.5 x 11 inch paper). If we estimate an average book to be about 250 pages and 6 x 9 inches (or less) for an average size, then a conservative estimate would be 50 books for every tree saved. The U.S. Department of Energy's statistic for the average number of trees per acre is about 700, which means you would have to read 35,000 books a year on your e-reader to save as much paper as a vegetarian does. If this vegetarian reads paper books, however, you would need to subtract how many he reads in a year to reach your final count – so if it's 20, you get 34,980.

That's a lot of eyestrain for anyone with an e-reader. Looking again at the above paragraph, if a person with an e-reader reads 50 books in a year, he is saving one tree. One. As compared to over 34,000. The point is not to push vegetarianism on readers, but to illustrate that the idealistic shout of "go paperless!" is almost baseless when you look into it – and it's getting tiresome to listen to. Anyone who gets an e-reader to "help the environment" is misinformed and has never researched this claim for themselves. Whatever paper they save is offset tenfold or more by the other negative impacts they create.

Using paper for books does not rape the rainforests or contribute to starvation; nor is it toxic like e-book components and does not adversely affect your health. Red meat is proven to be unhealthy and each time you eat a four-ounce burger made from rainforest beef, you allow about 55 square feet of rainforest to vanish. So if you save one tree per year with your e-reader and eat one burger, you're way behind in helping anything. Despite your best intentions, you are not helping the world very much by getting an e-reader. If that's your plan, do something else.

As we have established, rainforest trees are not used to create much of the world's paper. So to be fair, we should look at where the forests are where books currently come from. They are mostly in the United States, where no crisis exists regarding a shortage of trees. In fact, due to the paper industry, millions of new trees are planted every day by private landowners while fewer trees are being harvested for paper than those that are planted (many printing companies now use recycled paper). Currently, three to four times more trees are being planted than harvested in the United States.

Having more trees in the northern hemisphere compensates a bit for the outrageous harvesting and land stripping found in South America and other parts of the globe. If we were to suddenly go completely paperless in creating books, a large incentive to continue planting more trees would be gone. Sure, we could recycle all the old paper – but we could not do this indefinitely. With a continuing demand for paper in the U.S., based largely on printing paper books and other paper products, forests are growing and being managed for better sustainability. If we went completely paperless with books, we would be harming ourselves economically and even from an ecological point of view. An economic incentive is needed to keep growing trees, which we have. We are, in general, not mindful enough to maintain such a high output of new trees unless money can be made from them. This is a sad statement, but true.

Another argument against books is that paper uses too much energy to create them and other products, so we should cut back. This argument once held water, but times have changed. The U. S. pulp and paper industry now uses carbon-neutral *biofuels* to generate more than sixty per cent of its energy. It recovers its wood waste, chips, and left over pulping fibers and then consumes them for energy in the form of biofuels. Interesting fact: The largest producer and consumer of *renewable energy* is the U. S. pulp and paper industry. Yet, paper and those who use it (publishers) are being branded as ecological outlaws and attacked for "harming the environment." Nothing could be further from the truth. So the next time you buy a paper book, just know that you are doing your part to preserve forests and the jobs of those who maintain them in the U.S. It is a symbiotic relationship – the trees need you and you need the trees. Because of the way it works, buying paper books makes the whole thing sustainable. Not all of the new trees being grown will be turned into paper, but will be left alone in a sustainable way or used for other products. Many organizations outside of the paper industry are promoting tree growth or growing them.

Many printers, publishers and newspapers have become affiliated with a non-profit organization called the Green Press Initiative. In January 2012, they launched a certification program to encourage all those printing with paper to use fiber not sourced from ancient or endangered forests. Those doing the best job will get rewarded for their efforts. In the front of one book I recently read, which was published by Lantern Books in New York (*The World Peace Diet*, by Will Tuttle, Ph.D.), they posted a notice stating they had joined the Green Press Initiative. The notice also states that because of the type of recycled paper they used to publish the book, they saved 255 trees (40 feet tall and six to eight inches in diameter), 81 million BTU's of total energy, 724,105 pounds of greenhouse gases, 116,576 gallons of wastewater and 7078 pounds of solid waste. When you compare whatever might be left over here to what is used to create an e-reader, my money would be put on the paper book, hands down, regarding which product is "greener."

Some independent bookstores including The Book Tree in San Diego sell small "Grow a Tree" kits at their registers, available for purchase by every customer. Apple, cherry, various pines and even giant redwoods are available for $3.50 each. Additionally, many publishers and book companies have partnered with non-profit organizations and will plant a tree in developing countries that need it the most, often in Latin America and Africa, on behalf of every customer who buys a book from them. So awareness is being raised to help grow trees around the world.

Paper Books vs. E-Readers

Which is greener? Proponents of e-readers try to claim the crown, but most of the companies that make these devices fail to publicly disclose what they're made of or how the screens are manufactured. This point was brought out in an article from the *New York Times* from April 4, 2010, by Daniel Goleman and Gregory Norris called "How Green Is My iPad?" (http://www.nytimes.com/interactive/2010/04/04/opinion/04opchart.html) To solve the problem of this limited manufacturing data, they made a composite of the available information to form a reasonable estimate, and then made their calculations from there.

They chose to use what is called complete life-cycle assessment, which can determine the ecological impact of any product. They broke down the lives of e-readers and books into five life-cycle steps: Materials, Manufacture, Transportation, Reading, and Disposal.

Materials: One e-reader requires 33 pounds of minerals to be extracted from the earth. A book made with recycled paper requires about two-thirds of a pound of minerals. One e-reader needs 79 gallons of water to refine metals for the circuits, and to produce its batteries and wiring boards. A book needs only two gallons of water to make a slurry pulp that gets pressed and dried into paper.

Manufacture: An e-reader needs 100 kilowatt-hours to manufacture, while a book, whether it is made from recycled paper or not, needs just two kilowatt-hours. These same kilowatt-hours used for an e-book result in 66 pounds of carbon dioxide, while the greenhouse gases created for the production of a book are 100 times less than that. Also of consequence in relation to the manufacture of these items is the impact on health. Both e-readers and books emit gases like sulfur oxides and nitrogen during their manufacture, which can have damaging effects on health. These emissions are estimated to be 70 times higher with the making of an e-reader than with a traditional book.

Transportation: This is the grayest area, but at least there is some data to share. Driving to a bookstore round trip for ten miles causes about ten times the amount of pollution and resource depletion than what was needed to create one book. It is hard to make a direct comparison to e-books based on the *Times* data because the example given for e-books uses the equivalent of toxic impacts on health rather than resource depletion and pollution, so it is like comparing apples to oranges. Using toxic impacts, it is stated that driving to a store 300 miles away results in the equivalent of the toxic impacts on health used to make one e-reader. It also mentions that if a book ordered from the Internet is shipped to you 500 miles by air, it generates about the same amount of pollution as was needed to originally create the book. Although the information is interesting, inconsistent data makes this one area difficult to assess regarding a direct comparison.

Reading: Reading in daylight uses no energy except for the sun. If you read at night, however, a light bulb will use more energy in an hour or two than it does to charge an e-reader. What should also be considered and was not mentioned in the *Times* article, is that a book can be borrowed from a friend or library and read by hundreds of people in daylight without requiring power every time it is read.

Disposal: It was not specified whether books or e-readers create more toxicity during their disposal in the *Times* article, but only stated that both were guilty of doing so, through different means. The evidence seems to indicate, however, that paper has a more long-standing and developed ability to be recycled – although e-reading devices are beginning to close this gap.

The bottom line and conclusion to their findings is that you would have to read 40 to 50 e-books on your e-reader to equal the impact the device makes on mineral consumption, fossil fuels and water use. For global warming this figure rises to 100 e-books, and with the impact on human health, you would have to read about 75 e-books. Since the average person reads 4 books per year, it is clear that e-readers are nowhere near as "green" as some people would want us to believe. According to an Associated Press-Ipsos poll, 25% of all adults do not read any books at all. When you exclude these people, then the average reader in America reads about 7 books per year. If these happen to be e-books, then their e-readers would become "green" anywhere from 6 to 14 years, when going from the low to high impact figures. This figure goes down to 4 to 10 years if you use the 2006 Environmental Trends and Climate Impacts report, which says 3.1 billion books were sold in the U.S., which comes out to about 10 books per person.

Whichever way you look at it, however, the greener option is clearly with normal paper books.

The Legacy of Books

Books and people have been tied closely together for centuries. Most people believe the earliest known printed book was by Gutenberg in the 1450's, but it was actually printed in China on a block press in around 868 CE. The book was *The Diamond Sutra*, and copies are still being printed today – in English and other languages. It contains the main tenets of the Buddha's final teachings, so those who believe the Gutenberg Bible came first will have to look to Buddhism instead. It is believed that printed books may have been generated even before 868, but *The Diamond Sutra* is the earliest one we know of. It is believed the block press was replaced by movable type in China around 1041 by Bi Sheng, pre-dating Gutenberg's movable type by about four centuries. It was made out of Chinese porcelain and could do most everything Gutenberg's press did, but slower. Gutenberg can be credited with inventing the first full-blown printing press, which did things faster than anything that came before it.

Centuries of book printing followed, creating an explosion of information and the gift of knowledge to the masses. The Gutenberg printing press has been declared the single most influential invention for the benefit of mankind that we have ever had. And now we want to throw it out the window in exchange for a bunch of new gadgets that cannot and will not ever match it in importance. It is this writer's prediction that if we continue on this path and supplant normal book printing with electronic devices, we will later regret it as a serious mistake. Let us hope that we remain aware enough to value what we have, and never reach this point in time.

In 1971 the first e-book (The Declaration of Independence) was created by a student at the University of Illinois, and was downloaded by six people. Things grew a little bit and by the late 1980's, it was announced that by the year 2000 all paper books would be gone and everything would be in the form of e-books. They forgot one important fact that persisted throughout the 90's and into the 2000's. People in general have always *hated* e-books – until just recently. The year 2000 came and went without any significant change whatsoever. People ignored e-books. In the year 2000 most people still did not know what an e-book was, or did not care to know about them.

Clever people came along and tried to improve the technology in order to make money. Which they did. The technology has gotten better and is good for some people – even great. But the majority of people still do not desire them. They must get sold on the gadget, first. Many of those saying how great e-books are, are proponents who have an investment in the technology. They are trying to convince you to buy a gadget that they happen to be selling. At the same time, we must be fair to them and congratulate all those in the industry who have invested in the technology, improved it, and marketed it. E-books have caught on and they are here to stay. Those selling the technology have done an admirable job with marketing and development. They had to work hard at it and have *created* the demand, rather than it having been a demand to begin with. And people have responded.

All ideas, no matter what level they are on, must be marketed properly before they can be effective. There are some e-book proponents that may be angry about this book and my assertion that advanced marketing techniques played a huge role in their acceptance. The fact is that e-books were once repulsive to the vast majority of people during the 1990's and early 2000's. They were just too foreign for people to embrace and for many this will always be the case. *Virtually nobody wanted them.* Now that a respectable number of people actually want e-readers shows that people have accepted the hype – and created the demand. Now that sales are moving, improvements are being made to e-readers, which make them more appealing to those who prefer technical gadgets.

When you put an e-book side by side with a real book and ask someone to choose one to read from, most people will still choose the printed book. The printed book is simple. It is warm. It invites the reader in a more charming and personal way. There is a *connection* to the reader. It is not a cold gadget with buttons. Buttons are an insult to the integrity of a book. Those who need buttons to read a book while forsaking the tactile sensation of turning real pages are losing the complete experience of reading.

Turning books into electronic bytes is a grave reflection on society. Technology, science and culture have become so intertwined that there is no room left for *literature*. Think about it. The magic and beauty of literature, if it could speak, may not want to be forced into a corner by technology, and become subservient to things like bytes, downloads, and software upgrades. The spirit of literature does not want to die, hidden inside an Internet "cloud" or trapped under the metal hinges of any kind of device.

The Three Biggest Myths about E-books

1. **Printed books will soon be obsolete because of e-books.** Not true, despite constant claims from the e-book community that this will happen. E-books currently compose a small percentage of the sales market, with most e-books sold being best selling titles and fiction in the genres of romance, mysteries, detective novels and spy thrillers. Beyond these areas, comparatively little sells in e-book format at the current time. To help predict the future, let's look at music, which has had CDs on the market longer than e-books. Everyone predicted CDs would go by the wayside. But today, half of all music sales are still CDs. E-books will probably never command as much as 50% of book sales – but if it ever reaches this level, it will take far longer for it to happen than it did with music. Printed books drive e-book sales rather than the reverse, and this will be the case for many years to come. One significant pattern has become evident. A number of popular new titles sold very few e-books until the paper versions sold out. Only then did e-book sales jump to any significant degree. And reviewers often avoid e-book files.

Most of those who deal in e-book reviews only – the web-based book reviewers – still want to see and hold a printed version of the book rather than relying on just the e-book.

2. **Publishers, distributors, wholesalers and bookstores will no longer be needed because authors can now write, produce and sell their books directly to readers electronically.** All of these companies will continue to perform the exact same functions for e-books that they have doing for printed books all along. The primary function they perform is the selling of the book. Writers are generally better at writing, and are by no means experts in marketing. It takes special skills to match content with the right audience. Writers prefer to go on to their next book project, rather than dropping their main purpose in life and trying to become marketers. Some are good at it, but to be good at it you need to devote enough *time* to hone the craft of marketing and make the numerous contacts (and nurture them) that is required to succeed. In today's competitive market, a book is hard to lay out, design, market and publicize. If you want to make a living as a writer, you need a support system that has expertise in these areas. If you do not have this support system you may continue to get your books published easier than you have ever done before, but hardly anyone will read your material. Being a "published writer" will soon be a meaningless phrase since you will be offering just one of about a million new books per year, published and posted on the Internet by writers and digital "vanity presses" that have no marketing skills whatsoever. The trick is to be a good enough writer to be considered as a commodity by genuine "support system" companies. Young, cocky writers are coming up saying – often with great disrespect – that they can do it all themselves and be successful, but are in for a rude awakening. Legitimate publishers, distributors and wholesalers are here to stay.

3. **The new tablets and reading devices, with all their bells and whistles, are the wave of the future and will control how people read.** The new reading devices are impressive forms of technology, which is true. But it is and always will be the

content that inspires us to read. This is the mistake we are making now. We have become enamored with the technology and desire it because it is so new and clever. Readable book content now has a new option of being placed on a different background after a few hundred years, dependent on electrical circuitry and various gadgets instead of simple paper. The gadget is a novelty and nothing more. The *content* is the ruling feature and reflects our passions, our emotions, and what makes literature great. It is *not* the device. It is about the content. The content in e-book form is invisible until you turn the device on – so it is hard to focus on something that is not even visible or solid unless you focus on the device. The device is not the content. You can hold a book up and everyone knows there is content in there connected to one particular book, based on its cover. In contrast, hold up a reading device. To begin with, people don't even know if it's a book reader, a phone, or what it's really for in many cases. You might be able to say there's content in it, but no one can really see it unless you turn it on. We are disconnected, or removed from the important content, by one extra step. Devices are being noticed, however, because of the novelty involved. It takes far more time and knowledge to read great content than to play around with the cool features of these mass-produced gadgets. The device makers want you to be more concerned with their gadgets. Those who are more concerned with great content, and a more direct connection to it, will usually prefer a normal printed book.

Digital Hype

We live in an age of gimmicks, gizmos and gadgets – and it's only getting worse. The human race continues to prove how clever it is by creating all kinds of things we do not really need. We are being told that we need these things by large marketing agencies that will make money from you if they do their jobs well enough and convince you to buy their *junk*. Television commercials consist of a long parade of gimmicks that insults the intelligence of most people. The average consumer is being constantly barraged by ads begging you to buy things by intentionally being cute, stupid, nostalgic, funny – but very rarely intelligent or *logical*. People buy things out of impulse, not from clear, logical thinking. Marketing people know this. Enter the e-book reader. Nobody wanted e-books for the longest time, but finally, in the age of twitter, people are beginning to buy them.

Those who own e-books are less likely to read them because of the old adage, "out of sight, out of mind." They are easily forgotten. And those who do read their e-books usually read less from them than if they were physical books. More people will buy an e-book for research purposes and search out tidbits of information from them, rather than sit comfortably with it like an actual book and form more of a relationship with it. People generally spend more time engaged with real books.

It is easier to amass large collections of e-books because they are invisible, so you can have thousands of them. But reading them all is a very daunting task. Buying a physical book and carrying it around with you makes a statement. You are telling people, in effect, "I really like this one book. In fact, I like it so much, I am willing to carry it around, as a single volume, and give it the respect it deserves while I am reading it."

This is the ultimate compliment that you can pay a book.

The New Playing Field

Knowing the entire history of the book leads those who appreciate them to the hopeful conclusion that e-books are nothing but a passing fad. This will not prove to be true. E-books are here to stay. At the time of this writing their impact is still not great – but growing fast. Their sales comprise about 17% to 20% of the entire book market revenue of $80 billion dollars when it was hovering at about 5% just over a year ago. Studies show that the majority of those sales are for the major "best seller" books (from a comparison of print and e-book best seller lists generated by various retailers, combined with Simba Information). Therefore the vast majority of smaller, independent publishers that do not publish best sellers do not need to worry as much about e-books.

Only 12 companies publish the bulk of best selling titles, leaving the rest of the paper book market far less affected. The biggest publishers with the biggest budgets have pushed e-books to try and get a jump on their competition, but everyone else (meaning smaller publishers) don't care as much – at least not right now. The bigger giants of the publishing world have more use for e-readers and tablets than the smaller publishers do. Many small publishers have invested thousands of dollars into converting their titles into e-books, but have still not seen a return on the investment. Sales are being made, but conversion services can charge very high rates. It may take some time for smaller companies to recoup their initial investment if, in fact, they were able to make it.

People with short attention spans or those who need quick snippets of information from many different books will benefit the most from e-books. Those who are obsessed with technical gadgets will still buy them as well, although others will lose interest in the novelty of the devices and return to standard books. Many like myself have already done so.

Some who read for longer durations, from about 30 minutes or more at a time, often complain of eyestrain from reading on a computerized device – even from the newer, so-called "non-glare" screens. The output resolution on many of these devices is lower than that of a printed page in normal light. These devices can strain the eyes. For many, it is easier to process information from a steady source of normal light that is reflected off a printed page. As mentioned earlier in this book, studies suggest that more information is retained from reading from a normal book as opposed to using an electronic device of any kind.

Additional evidence exists to support achieving more clarity and comprehension from reading normal books. When reading from a computer one must process a variety of audio and visual information not found in standard books including hyperlinks, various audio tones, ads and the visual distraction of operating keys and buttons to continually access the text. In accordance with the level of extra activity, fMRI scans show more areas of the brain being activated. fMRI stand for functional magnetic resonance imaging, and is a way of measuring brain activity. When a normal book is being read, these additional areas remain quiet. As one reads, this quieting effect is similar to what is achieved through meditation – which is also known to focus the mind. More reflection and processing occur in this brain state. But when reading from a computer or electronic device, the brain generally moves too quickly or in too many different directions for the information to take root as effectively.

A team of researchers from the University of Washington presented results of a year-long study in May of 2011 showing that students found printed books to be more flexible and support a wider range of reading and learning styles than e-books. In general, students found e-readers to be cumbersome and ill-suited to their needs, suggesting that e-readers are clearly flawed as replacements for traditional textbooks.

Another study was completed in late 2010 by the University of California Libraries, which shared the results of their large e-textbook pilot program. They surveyed over 2500 student, with 58% of the respondents stating they used e-books for their academic work. This likely means that 42% of them chose not to use e-books at all. The majority of all three groups who did use e-books – graduates, undergraduates and faculty – said they preferred printed books instead. Those who preferred e-books generally did so when they needed to quickly find a certain fact or passage. Printed books were generally preferred for focused and attentive study. The primary complaint about e-books was the difficulty experienced in learning, concentrating and retaining information.

What is especially disturbing is that politicians had begun to propose changes in education policy without considering or waiting for the results of such studies. In 2010 Governor Rick Perry of Texas proposed that standard books should be abolished in favor of e-books and in 2009 then-California Governor Arnold Schwartzenegger said basically the same thing, dismissing printed books as being outdated. Printed books have been removed from the library of a private high school in Massachusetts and in 2011 the Florida Legislature passed a bill that will effectively remove textbooks from the entire state's schools by 2016 and replace them with digital editions.

I must inform a friend of mine about this, since he is working on a book called _Rush to Stupidity_ and am sure he will not hesitate to include this. This neglect is truly our culture's greatest current achievement in its rush to stupidity – and we can only hope that these and other studies will put a dose of patience and reconsideration back into the equation.

I must thank Nicholas Carr and his blog, "Rough Type," for this source material, and highly suggest reading two of them in particular for more information: "E-textbooks Flunk an Early Test," from May 12, 2011, found at www.roughtype.com/?p=1478, and "Another Study Points to Advantages of Printed Textbooks," from June 27, 2011, found at www.roughtype.com/?p=1496. He also wrote an excellent article (an update of the "Another Study" blog) for the Dallas Morning News dated August 5, 2011, titled "Schools Should Beware the E-book Bandwagon;" www.dallasnews.com/opinion/sunday-commentary/20110805-nicholas-carr-schools-should-beware-the-e-book-bandwagon.ece.

Signs of a Passing Fad

Yes, e-books are here to stay but in some ways are similar to the fad of astro-turf. Professional sports stadiums switched to using artificial grass in the 1970's and '80's because it was "easier" to maintain and sped up the games, making things happen faster for the enjoyment of spectators. E-books are similarly "easier" to maintain than a physical collection of books and access to them becomes faster through these new devices.

With astro-turf, it was found that over time, the careers of the players were being shortened. It was unhealthy to play on astro-turf, creating more knee and leg injuries because there is no natural softness to the artificial grass. It was almost like playing on cement.

The artificial grass also retained heat more than natural turf, literally baking the players like they were in a frying pan while trying to play the games. The fans were being entertained with faster moving games, the owners were saving money on the maintenance of natural grass, but the players were miserable, getting overheated, injured more often, and their careers were sometimes cut short. When star players are lost, fewer people attend games and money is lost. Hotter stadiums made it more uncomfortable for the fans as well as players – another reason to stay at home.

The users of e-books are experiencing this same type of "speed-up." Of course the unhealthy aspects operate on a lesser scale, but it seems they are there. Most voracious readers using a computerized device cannot go past a certain point due to eyestrain and in some cases, computer vision syndrome (CVS), which is not healthy. Being faster or "easier" is not necessarily better. And for reasons outlined elsewhere in this book, it is actually more costly, in the long run, to employ e-books and e-readers instead of just buying a regular book.

It took time, but most sports team owners have learned their lessons and removed artificial grass from their stadiums (some of these "grass" companies have now turned their marketing strategies toward normal homeowners who are too lazy to mow their lawns). This may not be the perfect analogy – comparing e-books to astro-turf – but enough similarity exists for the analogy to be drawn.

Purists will always choose a normal book, and not burden themselves with the overload of device and software choices. Why burden yourself with extra details when you can just pick up a book? Standard books have been perfected over centuries. Nevertheless, if an electronic version of anything can be imagined, they will try to build it.

With standard books there have been awards given out for well over a hundred years. Today, there are at least 275 prestigious book awards given out worldwide on a yearly basis. I recently saw a picture of a book award winner – an older author flanked by two beautiful women, proudly holding up his award-winning book. Question: What do you hold up if you win an e-book award? A little plastic device? What happens at these award ceremonies if everything converts to e-books someday? Will everyone ignore each other and stare into computer screens to admire the winning entries? Like they do nowadays to read these products?

I suppose you could hold up a tablet with the cover displayed on it – but the point is, it's not a real book. This is like winning a fishing tournament and then holding up a *picture* of your winning fish rather than the real thing. Or entering a vegetable or pumpkin growing contest by showing up and entering your picture of it, rather than the real item. Computer generated pumpkins or other vegetables do not qualify in real life growing contests, so why are we considering computer-generated books as legitimate substitutes for books? When you go to a restaurant, do you eat the menu? Or do you prefer real food?

But today, even real food is under attack in the same way, being created in substitute ways for profit. Many foods have become genetically modified because they are faster, easier and more profitable to produce. Genetically modified organisms (or GMOs) are produced in a laboratory, so that many grains and vegetables and no longer real, but fake. They are not real food in the same way e-books are not real books. The same general information – or substance – is there, but appears in a counterfeit way. GMOs have not been tested over long periods of time, and many health experts claim they are very harmful to humans – with some tests on animals showing negative results. But the big corporations that own the patents on these GMOs and are pushing them onto the public claim they are fine, despite the fact that many European countries have banned them. Those pushing e-books onto the public also claim that e-books are better. Numerous studies are beginning to show otherwise. For some people this really may be the case but despite all the hype, they are not better for everyone. That is the reason this book was written. Not everyone is embracing e-books, despite the big marketing blitz that is under way. No thank you, is the resounding cry from a large segment of people.

Do those fake electronic cigarettes *really* satisfy a smoker?

Is electronic text messaging really needed when you can just pick up a phone and call someone, and more quickly, like in the old days?... *Hello?*

Are GMO foods really healthy and safe to consume?

The Pitfalls of Progress

Are we complicating things too much? Are we forcing new things upon each other that we really don't need just because someone invented it as a nifty new gadget?

Let's take a look at technological progress in general. From the 1980's, things like cell phones and computers were huge improvements over the way things were done before. They are, without question, great advances that benefit us all. However, when a myriad of additional applications (or "apps") get heaped upon these devices, it waters them down. There are so many apps these days it will make your head spin.

Diversity is one thing, but when you start replacing normal phone calls with texting, and normal books with electronic ones, we start moving into the arena of needlessness. Sure, some people want these things because it represents a "new thing" that a gadget can do, and they are fascinated with such novelty. At some point, the novelty will wear off, but those who produced the new app or device don't care, because they will have made their money. Some will argue that texting is good because it allows you to send messages when a person is unable to answer their phone. To this I say, *Leave a message*. It takes less time. The only thing we have in order to live in this world is *time*. If you want to waste it while trying to type on tiny little keys and pressing various buttons, which takes far longer than just *speaking*, so that people can make a profit from you, then that is your choice. I must agree that there are some useful applications for texting. They include 1) sending messages to people who don't want to hear from you or hate you – and would never otherwise answer their phone; 2) sending (or receiving) answers to tests in school to help people *cheat*; or 3) you can ask people things you would normally not wish to in a face to face setting (like asking for a date), which will help stunt the social skills of an entire generation of young people. Distancing people from each other and creating social dysfunction is a major side effect of the technological prescriptions you voluntarily administer to yourself and others through the nifty, modern gadgets being made available today.

But back to e-books. To a certain degree, they represent themselves as a fad. When the large wave of interest in them as a novelty subsides, e-books will still not disappear. They are clearly not a passing fad. They will not go the way of the pet rock of astro-turf. There will always be a place for them. The important thing to remember, however, is simplicity. Paper books have been around for hundreds of years and exist in a trusted, simpler form than all these modern electronic versions. E-book proponents may argue that nothing is more simple and compact than a small electronic file that cannot even be seen unless you open it. What could be simpler than that? On the surface, this does seem rather simple, but when you examine all the trappings that go with this "simple" file, a whole world of complexity, costs and confusion opens up (you might want to reread the front cover of this book, for example, as a brief refresher).

Normal paper books should not be cast aside in the rush for answers in this exploding electronic age. Because smaller circuits have been devised to allow portability for virtually any type of information exchange or storage, people have become too dependent upon electronic devices. Electronic applications have been created for virtually every form of information mankind needs, from ridiculously trivial to the greatest of importance, in an attempt by manufacturers to get their devices into the hands of as many groups of people as possible.

Devices have become multi-functional in order to steal the market from those with individual functions – for example, cell phones can not only "text" messages as an alternative form of communication, they can also access the Internet, send and receive emails, play music and videos, and serve as an e-book reader. There's a new "Galaxy" device that operates as a phone and a fully functional tablet. Combining services into an "all-in-one" device creates the demand that companies have been striving for. A "do-it-all" device, however, often does a number of things in a mediocre fashion, as opposed to devices that are designed strictly to perform one thing – and to do it well. This is a consistent pattern that has appeared in electronic devices for many years. Dedicated fax machines, for example, were built strictly for that purpose and reached an extremely high operating quality in the 1990's. Then companies started combining features, so they began to serve as multi-functional copiers, scanners and fax machines. All the reviews for the multi-function equipment, including those from the best reviewers like Consumer Reports, showed them to be inferior, across the board, to equipment designed and built to perform specific functions. We have the same problem today.

It is the shotgun effect. Example: If you are alone in the wilderness and a hungry lion spots you from a hundred yards away and heads toward you, using a shotgun from that distance will do nothing. But a well aimed rifle shot will stop the lion in its tracks before it can get anywhere near you. In much the same way, society has traded away its expertise to hone in and make great products for specific purposes, for a slide into mediocrity using the "shotgun" effect.

Technology companies would prefer you do many things less effectively on one device, rather than be limited with one thing done well. Single-functioned items sell for less money than ones with multi functions.

E-book readers are heading in this direction. An October, 2011 article on Yahoo News predicted ten technological things that would be gone by 2020. One of them is e-readers. It is predicted that multi-function "tablets," like the iPad, would replace them entirely since reading books will be an included function. So it's the same story repeating itself, with companies bundling functions together in an effort to appeal to everyone.

This is good news for paper books, because books are individual physical objects. You cannot "multi-function" them because they are not electronic. They are simple, and many, many people prefer them that way. If one of the many functions on an electronic device *malfunctions*, you usually trash the entire device and must buy a new one. And they cost more. Tablets, due their more elaborate nature, will always be more expensive than smaller e-readers, so it will become more prohibitive, cost-wise, to buy them – especially for people who would prefer to read a simple book, and not involve themselves with additional functions just to do so. So the paper book is not dead; nor will it die. It just asks intelligent people with clear purpose to notice this fact and act accordingly.

Exposure to EMFs

Electronic devices create EMFs (electromagnetic fields), including the radiation from cell phones that studies have attributed to brain cancer. E-readers can also operate wirelessly and your phone may one day double as your e-reader – if it doesn't do so already. Some of the newer e-readers use wireless communications by default, so it is a good idea, if you have one, to turn the wi-fi off when you're not using it. Although standards have been developed for EMF radiation levels, it has not been scientifically determined what a safe level really is. It is up to you to determine what is safe based on how your body reacts around these energies.

Electronic signals are bombarding you at this very moment, although it is clearly safer when the source is further away from you. We are bathing the planet with EMFs to the point where every day, 4.6 billion people are on their cell phones. If the Earth (Gaia) is a living being, she must be fighting to retain her normal vibrational frequency. The long-term effects of these frequencies are unknown but at least, on a personal level, you can distance yourself from direct exposure. If you want to read e-books in the future and only multi-purpose gadgets are available, you'll be coerced, out of convenience, into using a cell phone that would transmit EMFs directly into your brain.

I recently met a young man named B. James, who chose not to be more specific with his name. He provided me with a list of 16 patent numbers (he had many more) for inventions that would allow various forms of manipulation on humans through EMFs. Anyone with an electronic device would be vulnerable. The list includes speech pattern processing to determine your psychological make-up, nervous system manipulation via EM fields, and a silent subliminal messaging system. It is not my intention to cause paranoia, but hidden things like Carrier IQ have already been uncovered in devices, as mentioned earlier.

Staying Focused

Your mind is your greatest asset; it is the one tool in life you have that needs to be focused, rather than scattered. Reading a standard, printed book will keep your mind sharp and focused on the task at hand. Your book will not interrupt you with an email chime, a built-in phone ring, or an alert to charge your battery. You will retain the information better and will appreciate the peace and knowledge that you will reap as a direct reward.

Some people pride themselves in being able to do more than one thing at a time. They called it "multi-tasking," and wear the label as a badge of honor. But when you test them on what they've accomplished – after they have finished their tasks – their answers will almost always be less informative and prove less retention than someone who was focused on doing only one task. They are more concerned with finishing all their tasks (and bragging about it), rather than excelling at one thing in a focused, dedicated manner. After all, we just don't have the *time* anymore to do just one thing. If we want to succeed in life, we are being given the false impression that we must race around like crazy people and do as many things as possible in a limited period of time. At least this is what society is trying to burden you with. *Don't play that game.* You don't have to. The very best and most accomplished, successful people are those who devoted themselves fully to learning an art or skill so well that they eventually become too good to be ignored. But society continues to pull people in more and more different directions and makes this harder to accomplish. If you love something, stay focused on it.

We are barraged by so many things these days that there is much less time for us to live up to all of the commitments, both in time and money, that is demanded from us. People have become "scatterbrained" from the demand and will do their best to accomplish what they still can under any circumstances (multi-tasking). This is why it is illegal in most places throughout the world to drive a car and be on a cell phone (or be texting) at the same time. You cannot focus effectively on the main task at hand if you are scattered. In these cases, it is dangerous, and people have lost their lives. But because they can get away with it, car manufacturers like Chrysler, Audi and Cadillac, among others, have begun offering Internet access in the dashboards of new cars. The New York Times ran an article called "Driven to Distraction," warning of the dangers (http://www.nytimes.com/2010/01/07/technology/07distracted. html?pagewanted=all), dated Jan. 6, 2010, and called it "the pursuit of profit over safety." This means we have another great place to read our online e-books or surf the net (should traffic conditions warrant it, according to some of the owner's manuals). Nobody in their right mind attempts to read a normal book while driving – but build it into the dashboard and temptation will obviously rear it's ugly head. What else could possibly be the result? Instead of reading your book in a "cloud," you might end up floating in one, playing a harp.

Some car manufacturers have begun to employ a "blind spot" detector in the driver side mirrors or new cars, to save lives by detecting anything that might be in your blind spot and generating an audible warning before you make a bad mistake. Before putting Internet access in any vehicle, every car on the road should be equipped with one of *these*, rather the Internet access.

Many times, people will want something because no one else they know has it, and having one will make them special, or unique. At least until it gets old. If it's "new," people will rush to get it without determining how practical – or safe – it really is. Those who make such products are not concerned with practicality or in some cases, safety. They are concerned only with sales and the public, in large part, has been trained by them to be consumers of all things "new."

Chapter Four

The Post-Literate Society

This phrase was used by Ted Rall in an article from the March 15, 2011 newspaper, The Progressive Populist (which reports interesting news that you will not often find elsewhere). His article was called "Pirate This Book." In it, he expressed concern for the printed word being under siege and mentioned that the next time you walk past one of the empty buildings that once held a Borders bookstore, you might ask, Are we becoming a post-literate society?

The mere fact that this question comes up, points strongly toward the answer being "yes." It is my contention that we are already there.

Public libraries, the flagships of learning for many communities, are closing branches, reducing hours and laying people off despite a 20 per cent increase in demand for their usage. Many have downsized and are converting to digital format books – not because they want to, but because it will save enough money to allow them to stay open. It is better to stay open and offer something downsized or inferior than to be completely out of business.

There are many signs that we are in a post-literate society. E-books are often not read or used just once and forgotten because they are not physical objects. Another good example is Twitter. Twitter allows you to share limited messages with others on the Internet and to "follow" those whose messages you like. Millions of people are stumbling all over each other, just for the chance to "follow" others (who might have answers that they don't), and trade extremely short messages of little or no substance. The space limitations do not allow it. You are allowed to type up to 140 characters. The art of conversation gets totally lost because of the immense lag times in getting a response (if, by chance, you get one), and by competing with hundreds, or even thousands of others who have also injected themselves into the exchange. This is like walking up to someone in a crowded room, blurting out something for all to hear, then walking away. If someone responds, fine. But you said your piece and that's all that counts. Relying on Twitter for the primary part of one's interactions with the world – and there are such people – help to create a society of individuals that do not know how to interact fluently in face-to-face situations. And those who are anti-social to begin with flock to places like Twitter and Facebook, which only reinforces their distant behavior.

Today, the time needed to physically interact with others has drastically shortened. This extremely shallow window of time and space, found on computerized devices, is all that most people have these days for any kind of information gathering. Libraries are closing, where people have traditionally gone and spent lengthy, focused time engaged in important research. This is becoming less possible while, at the same time, Twitter is exploding. According to Ted Rall, Twitter's estimated value is $3.7 billion, while the esteemed magazine, *Newsweek*, was "recently sold for a buck (plus a promise to assume tens of millions in debt)." It seems pretty clear that our priorities have become skewed. We have sunk into a post-literate era, but few would admit it – or even care to admit it. At least not until more of the inevitable repercussions begin to surface.

E-books are part of this social mix, and fit in by supporting this type of behavior. People are less inclined to read a book that is stored away on a hard drive and is invisible to the human eye. The ability of computers and hand-held devices to store thousands of books as an alternative to a standard bookshelf, encourages people to purchase and collect e-books faster than they could read them. The ads online often claim you can download these books instantly and wirelessly, in seconds. Yet, will people bother to read them?

Paper books, which require more space to store due to their size, encourage people to notice them, talk about them and yes, even read them and pass them on, so they can make room for more reading material. It is much easier to forget about an e-book after one has downloaded it. I've often overheard conversations of people bragging about how many e-books they have in their "libraries" – however, no one has ever mentioned how many of them they have actually read.

The point of having books is to read them. The used book business serves the purpose of allowing people to pass books on to others that they have actually *read*. However, there is no such thing as a used e-book. I would be willing to bet that the percentage of used paper books that have been read in any given year far exceeds, by a landslide, all the e-books that have ever been read in their entire history (not just purchased, but actually read from beginning to end). Those who attempt to read an e-book are more inclined to be distracted by links, Internet access, or the mountain of other titles they have access to, and as a result only read a portion of the book, if anything. This contributes to the *dumbing down* of society. Young people, in general, are less educated and informed about important matters than at any time in the recent past, despite their being exposed to far more information than at any time in the past. This is an amazing quandary, created by technology. There will be those who will use the information available to them in this new electronic age and will become shining stars – beacons of information – but they will be exceptions, rather than the rule. The dumbing down trend already has us in its tight, dominating grasp.

Social networking through Twitter and Facebook has both positive and negative aspects. It is possible to meet many interesting people through these networks that would have never previously been possible. However, child molesters have successfully recruited young victims from the Internet and prison inmates have accessed their previous victims' social network files, printed out their information and sent them as veiled threats to parents or family members. The main concern, however, is more all-encompassing. People have amassed hundreds, and sometimes thousands of "friends" and followers on these networks, whom they have never met at all – yet call them friends. The word "friend" has taken on an entirely new meaning; a more haphazard version of the term, which may require a new meaning being added to its definition in modern dictionaries.

What do social networks have to do with e-books? They are both a reflection of the post-literate society. We had to create a new sub-definition for a "book" – an "e-book" to be precise – and add it to our modern dictionaries. An e-book is a colder, more distant form of the real thing, like what the Wii has done to physical activity and what "friends" have done to social networking. It is a counterfeit of the real thing or, at the very least, something diminished in value. The value of an e-book is diminished because you don't often pay as much to get one, and it is not plainly visible unless you "open" it, making it easy to forget. Many new items are being presented to us by the advances of technology – and we end up paying more for the technology and *less* for the items that we should be focusing on. Our value gets transferred into the technology. We have begun to value the technology more than the knowledge it is meant to disseminate.

Something colder and more distant results as the final product, mainly because we are preoccupied with operating the technology to retrieve it! The information is presented in shiny plastic cases with lots buttons, tasks and noises, and separates you from genuine forms of warmth and experience. You did not come into life to be a slave to technology. You are here to *live life*, not to simulate it or be forced to reach further and further to access it. On many levels, this new technology robs you of tactile sensations that normally ground you in reality. For example, another feature that a real book offers is that, when reading, you hold the beginning part in your left hand and the ending in your right. You always know, as you are reading, where in the book you are at all times – how far there is to go before reaching the end. We are nearing the end in this book, and knowing this while reading can sometimes be useful.

The Importance of Handwriting

Another example of the post-literate society can be found in the state of Indiana (and possibly other states as well). It announced in 2011 that it has now abandoned teaching children penmanship in public schools, due to the prevalence of computers (Newsmax Magazine, Sept., 2011, "The Handwriting is On the Wall," by Theodore Dalrymple). What are we to make of this? Everyone's handwriting is unique. It is like a fingerprint of expression and provides each of us with a unique, distinguishing feature about ourselves. It is part of our identity. In his summary, Dalrymple states, "Those who learn to only write on a screen will have more difficulty in distinguishing themselves from each other, and since the need to do so will remain, they will adopt more extreme ways of doing so. Less handwriting, then more social pathology." This is not an absurd statement. We have already begun to see this pathology in elevated levels, like with Internet character defamation, or with physical bullying, which was never as vicious and widespread as it is today. Many young people have committed suicide because of it. The dependence on technology has created a rift between children, often preventing them from seeing each other as people with feelings, concerns and emotions, but as competitors to be beaten down under the mistaken illusion that it will increase the perpetrator's own standing among their peers. The evidence indicates that handwriting, when used for everything in school (without typing), creates a stronger personal identity for each and every student.

With the loss of handwriting, an additional concern is children having to endure a roomful of typing sounds during a test. How would you concentrate? Remember *libraries*? There's a reason why libraries are supposed to be quiet – but they are also becoming a thing of the past. Even with just a few people in a room, the collective sound of keyboards tapping would drive me crazy – but I suppose this happens everywhere now and children must learn to cope with it rather than fail their classes. The more thoughtful student, who is contemplative and must stop, periodically, to *think*, is most hurt by this. Under quiet circumstances they would be the best students, but enduring the anxiety of dozens of people making progress around you, while you struggle with your thoughts, trying to compete with their racket, can only make matters worse, increase the anxiety, and can contribute to their failure. In quieter surroundings some students would achieve the exact opposite and earn much higher grades. According to the Internet, a few law schools allow and even provide earplugs upon request for important tests, due to keyboard noise, but many other schools prohibit them – probably because certain transmitting devices that can relay answers may look similar.

Overcome by the allure of gadgets and technology, we have lost the value of simple things like handwriting. Your e-reader (if you have one) is, in most cases, multi-functional and allows you to type emails or text people. The manufacturers prefer to offer this so you will have more reasons to buy their product. As a result, many e-reading devices contribute to the lack of handwriting. When you handwrite notes or read from a printed book, you retain more of the information than if you typed it into a device and then read it from that device.

Evidence indicates that handwriting allows you to better execute and remember your ideas. See, for example, the article by Kevin Purdy from Dec. 4, 2011 called "The Pen is Mightier Than The Phone: A Case For Writing Things Out." This article now appears all over the Internet (people continue to share it). There's no way to tell what the original source was, but if you Google it within a reasonable time after this book's release, you should be able to find it. In it he says it is much better to carry a pencil or pen and a pad of paper because it is cheap and easy to do. Using paper also creates "a smoother path from your brain to the printed word, it saves you from task-switching overload, and it possibly makes the best to-do list." He also quotes efficiency consultant Marina Martin, who says, "Even the most fluid, thoughtful electronics introduce too much friction into the process of thinking, writing down, then thinking further out." When we get an idea, we have to find the electronic device, turn it on, open the word processing program, wait for it to boot up and, if it's a smaller device, you might need to adjust your font size and/or margins before typing anything in at all. By that time, you are lucky to remember anything.

Also cited in Purdy's article are the brain scans conducted by Virginia Berninger, a professor of educational psychology, which prove that by writing out your thoughts, they are "locked into place" and remembered more easily. As your hand creates each stroke in a letter, it activates a much greater part of the brain's working memory, thinking and language functions than with typing them. Other studies exist to support "stronger and lasting recognition" when information is handwritten. But the state of Indiana doesn't believe in teaching handwriting anymore, and possibly others, which is a complete and total shame.

When things are handwritten, one often gets the feeling that something has actually been *done* about a situation. The information does not disappear behind a blank screen when the device is shut off. You have created it and made it part of the real world that exists around you once you have written it down. On solid paper you can pick it up and see exactly how much you have done with it, and you do not have to scroll through screens to be reminded of what is there. It has been found that those with certain anxieties choose to release them by writing them down in the real world as opposed to tapping on keys or typing. In addition, many of the best self-help experts repeatedly have their clients *write down* what they wish to accomplish – and it has been found that a higher percentage of goals are actually realized when this method is employed.

E-Book Devices in the Post-Literate Age

E-book devices play a role in our turning away from more tactile tools for education, especially paper books, and studies show that we retain less data from their use. We may become more irritable and sleep less, as well, based on an *L.A. Times* article ("Reading on iPad Before Bed can Affect Sleep Habits") from April 24, 2010. Devices containing liquid-crystal screens like the iPad can inhibit the body's secretion of melatonin and disrupt the ability to sleep. For years people have read before bed as a way to "wind down" and relax, but these devices seem to create the exact opposite effect. In many other ways, e-books and e-readers play contributing roles in the post-literate age.

Chapter Five

Public Libraries

A good example of something of value being pushed aside by our society is the public library. They are disappearing, closing down, because people would rather sit at home and push buttons, too lazy to actually go and experience what a library is. The travesty is that future generations may never experience a library due to the laziness of our present generation.

Some may argue that it is the ingenuity of the present generation that should be the focus, and that we no longer need libraries because we are now "too smart" to access information in such an outmoded way. It is a big mistake to believe this – something that we, as a society, are trying to talk ourselves into because of budgetary restraints. To quote Antonino D'Ambrosio, from his Nov. 2011 *Progressive* magazine article, "Overdue Notice: Defend Our Libraries," he says, "In this age of the Internet and social media, some question the relevance of libraries, even declaring them obsolete. In reality, they are more important than ever."

We are allowing ourselves to be swept along by "progress" but the pace of it, especially in technological areas, has increased to the point where essential things can be mistakenly displaced before their importance is exhausted. We need to stop listening to all the hype and re-ground ourselves in a modality of simplicity – to at least maintain some fairness and practicality in our culture.

The health of our civilization, the depth of our awareness about the underpinnings of our culture, and our concern for the future can all be tested by how well we support our libraries. —Carl Sagan

A chapter on libraries is included because cutbacks and smaller budgets make e-books a threat to physical books, which most libraries depend on. Accessing information on the Internet is also a threat to these important institutions. There are many advantages a normal library has over the Internet. A great deal of information is found only in the library system and not on the Internet. Important academic papers and research materials found online are often available only by paid subscription, which can be costly, but this access can often be found through public libraries, for free. This is important to those on limited incomes. Many information sources found online have been abbreviated so contain only snippets of information, but you can often find complete, original sources in the library.

Much support can be found online for libraries. For example, CollegeOnline has an article called "16 Reasons Why Libraries and Librarians are Still Extremely Important," listing many advantages still held over the Internet (http://www.collegeonline.org/library/adult-continued-education/librarians-needed.html). It mentions that students have better test scores when they use the library for research instead of the Internet. This is no surprise when comparing this to the other test results and data referred to in this book – which also points to higher recall of material across the board when it is accessed in a normal book, rather than from a computerized screen. For other, additional, supporting information about libraries, see the CollegeOnline article.

Portability has made it convenient for us to avoid the library system. Electronic circuitry has gotten so small that most every creative super-nerd well versed in circuitry has patented some kind of portable electronic device and put it on the market. Which means you have to *squint* at it because it's so incredibly small and "convenient." And have you ever tried typing on one of those little texting devices, with keys so small that a lumberjack can hit every single key all at once, just by pressing down with his *thumb*? It is difficult to hold these devices in a comfortable way (as you would do with a normal book, for instance) because they are so small. When you add the screen glare that some of these things put out, you have to squint even more.

The Importance of Libraries

Although George Washington was considered the father of our country, the United States, Benjamin Franklin was considered the father of our libraries. In July of 1731 he and a group of friends opened The Library Company of Philadelphia, which continues to this day as a non-profit organization and has over 500,000 books. This tradition, however, is under attack from local governments nation-wide that are being forced to cut funds. Virtually ever major city has recently cut their budgets in some way and many have closed branches including New York City, which closed 14 of them and put about 300 people out of work. On the state level, 19 states cut funds to public libraries in 2011.

Despite the rampant cutbacks and closures of libraries, 31% of all Americans chose the public library as their favorite tax-supported service, according to a poll taken by the American Library Association. State and local budget-cutters find libraries an easy target, but often fail to correctly assess the economic impact libraries have. In general, libraries generate sizable profits and benefits to the community. For example, in the 2010 fiscal year the Free Library of Philadelphia created more than $30 million worth of economic value to the city and their invaluable resources had a direct and positive impact on more than 8600 local businesses, based on a study done by the University of Pennsylvania's Fels Institute of Government. Those with visions of replacing public library books with e-books and e-readers need to think again. You cannot replace entire, community-based institutions with hand-held pocket gadgets, despite all of the hype.

Accessing the Internet from within the library itself, however, is important. Many people depend on their library for Internet access, which they would not otherwise have. Libraries promote social interaction rather than having people funnel their attention toward a tiny screen, isolated in their homes. One of the great things about libraries is that you can find people with common interests and learn from them. You can make important contacts that can be more lasting and meaningful than if done from a distance, with the cold tools otherwise available. Libraries keep people connected to real books, as well as real people. In doing so, you are more inclined to learn the true art of *research*, rather than Googling things on a "hit or miss" basis. True research requires the use of indexes, cross-referencing and basic common sense. For example, when browsing the stacks or walking down an aisle, a magazine or newspaper headline could catch your eye that relates to your subject – one that would never be found in cyberspace or with a gadget. Asking a librarian for research tips on your subject can also bring a literal gold mine of results. Being surrounded by information and people who can help you access it can bring more useful information to a researcher than the Internet. Research papers will be more interesting because everyone else's research will say the same thing – having been sourced from the Net. As previously mentioned, higher test scores and grades have been shown to occur with people who use libraries as their main tool for research.

In 2011 the city of Oakland, California called for mass library closings due to budgetary cuts. The community responded by forming the Save Oakland Libraries coalition. They put on events, created a mock funeral procession and sponsored a "read-in" outside of City Hall that lasted for fourteen hours. Officials were shown the value of libraries and as a result, all fourteen branches in Oakland were allowed to remain open. This goes to show that some less inspired communities have lost an extremely valuable resource because they failed to act.

Many communities in rural areas or in areas less wealthy depend a great deal on their local library – especially for the children who need to learn good research skills or be left behind. Many jobs these days are advertised and applied for only through the Internet, so if you do not have access to a connection, you could lose out on a life-changing opportunity that you would be fully qualified for.

Being in your home or at a library and connecting to the Internet puts you in a setting where you can study and work. Accessing the Internet or your television from anywhere with a portable device is detrimental to social skills and can be a distraction to others in public, depending on the situation. Convincing people that they are empowered because they can connect to the Internet or a TV at any time and from any place, with a portable device, is a lie. You are *not* empowered when you promote a form of social breakdown, and are aiding and abetting in the *robbery* of an important form of cultural exchange. Libraries are social institutions that empower you because they do not isolate you. It doesn't matter who you are – you are not empowered by being isolated. We need each other, and we especially need the closeness and interaction that forms the fabric of our social structure. We are not islands; we are communities. So put your devices down and go to the library, get a real book, truly educate yourself and form some bonds at the same time.

These same bonds are created in bookstores as well. I have met two of the most important people in my life (at separate times) while browsing in a bookstore and striking up a conversation with them because of shared interests. It changed my life. Do *that* with an e-reader. Some may argue that it is done with computers all the time through social networking. But how is it possible to have a "friend" just by saying that you are, and never meeting in person? It is the shallow, post-literate society at work.

Sometimes, in a library or bookstore, you stumble across amazing things that you would have never found if otherwise engaged in isolation with your computer or e-reader. Physical exploration is fun; it can be an adventure. The only thing your e-reader or computer will do is spit out information in quantity that is often less specific than what you could find in a library. It will also gather information *about you* that you may not prefer, but at the library only you are the one gathering information. For example, oftentimes your viewed items and purchases are recorded and, based on what you have bought in the past, recommendations are made in a cold, technical manner on what it thinks you should buy or look at next. Many respond to these cues without even thinking for themselves. But your true thoughts and opinions matter more than past actions and the data associated with it. You have far more depth and meaning to be treated like a one-dimensional, predictable piece of data and you should respect yourself enough to provide your intellect and curiosity with proper avenues of stimulating exploration. Don't get lazy and allow yourself to be manipulated and exploited by a system that is designed to use you. You, instead, need to use the system more fully to your benefit and not allow the socially limiting features of technology rob you of this important dimension that exists within you – and within society itself.

Technology has been blinding you to the loss this social aspect, hoping you will not notice that it is quickly vanishing. As things stand today, social strength of communities will soon be gone – in large part removed with public libraries, which are traditional beacons for this in communities all across the country. Many technological companies are banking on the idea that you will indeed surrender the important social aspects of your community and your life in exchange for using all of their neat new bells and whistles.

I am not a Luddite, but a realist who is trying to keep you connected to the warmth of your own humanity. And your communities. Few have been able to put a finger on it, but there is a certain "distancing" going on with e-books and all other related technology that we should be aware of. It is subtle, but it is there. Some people are bothered by it; others are not. But at least you should be aware of it – which is one of the reasons for this book. You do not want to wake up someday after many years of experiencing less and less social interaction, which was slowly and imperceptibly removed from your life because things were made "easier" for you, only to discover that you have evolved into an entirely different creature – living your life with relationships that are messed up or non-existent, and you don't know why. With that possibility in mind, you may want to *avoid it from the start.*

Chapter Six

Newspapers

Newspapers are covered in this book because they share the same digital dilemma as books. However, newspapers have taken a far more drastic hit and are being forced to adapt. Newspapers are moving into new areas of reporting and distribution out of necessity. Book publishers looking to the future should be aware of how these options are being worked with by newspapers, should the same necessities surface.

The entire world of news has changed due to computers, e-readers, smartphones and other similar devices. If you are a news junkie or have a job that requires instant access at all times, then a portable e-reading device is essential. Many others access news this way because of the convenience. When news is accessed electronically, it puts a big dent in the sale of physical papers. Television news has always been free, but it never made a large enough impact to effect newspaper sales on a serious level. Years ago, other news sources were not around. It was either one or the other – newspapers or television –but most people used both. When asked why they didn't get a paper, some people would say they got their news from television only. But when you compare the level of information between newspapers and television, you get only the tip of the iceberg from TV. Anyone serious about their news always got (and still get) the local paper – and additional ones known for extensive coverage like *The New York Times, Washington Post, USA Today, Los Angeles Times* or the *Boston Globe*.

People still get newspapers today, but there are fewer to choose from. They are vanishing. Paper books will always remain timeless because they involve lessons from history, longer stories or extensive research material. However, news typically lasts for a day – unless it is a larger story with a "continuation," which can create day-to-day coverage. Because news is generally so short-lived, it is easy to destroy its value if others wishing to report it can access it as quickly as newspaper reporters – if not faster – which is what has happened with the advent of computers and Internet access. The jobs that go with traditional news organizations also get destroyed by making news available for free in the many places we find it today. There are too many easy-access channels of information today in order for news to remain a commodity.

The Internet is the biggest purveyor of free news and information today – and it covers far more ground than papers ever did, being, of course, the "world-wide web." To stay in the game of distributing news, papers have had to branch out, away from paper. In order to survive, most newspapers now offer digital versions of their stories, available through the Internet. The only problem is that virtually anyone can become a news reporter today without having any of the hard-earned qualifications previously worked for by professional journalists and news people. Just find a good story, jump on twitter and post the link. Or take the latest news story of your personal interest on a daily basis and post it with a little more depth and opinion by becoming a blogger. Or a podcaster. Or just throw the neatest, newest stories up on a specially made, news-based website, which you could practically build overnight. If you have the time to maintain it, you can compete with the biggest news agencies in the world. You can also set up a kind of automatically generated newsletter/newspaper using information you get from like-minded friends or followers. All of is this accessible on your e-reader or smartphone. Twitter is now considered to be the new AP, with CNN, Fox News or whatever else you need, all rolled into one. You can set it up to receive tweets from any news providers that interest you. Since Twitter reports only links, you have to bounce around a bit and open them to get what you want. Many newspapers are right there in the Twitter game, and people often prefer their tweets and stay loyal to these papers due to their long-standing trust and reputation.

Journalism isn't dying; it's exploding – but in different forms. So newspapers must become innovative and exploit these new forms in ways that will benefit their organizations. The news business is now driven purely by technology. This opens the door to technology geeks who like to report news, but have no professional experience. Professional journalists can still shine, but they have more competition. Non-professional bloggers have fewer resources for news than professionals – they mostly surf around the Net and share what they can find. But reliable sources and professional contacts will usually deal with established organizations like newspapers when choosing where to break a story. Papers often have long-standing relationships with many of the best sources. Once the best news is received, whether exclusively or not, the next step is to present it to more people than anyone else and make a profit. Newspaper companies can still do this if they are creative and hard working in their approach.

Unlike books, newspapers depend on advertising. Currently, the majority of advertising revenue still comes from printed versions of the paper. An advertiser wants to see something solid and more "in the world" when advertising their products. Online, it is far easier to scroll or click a button, and then the ad is gone forever. With a newspaper, the ad is still there when you put the paper down and it remains in your field of view whenever you pick the paper up again. One page from a physical newspaper has a far greater field of view than with a small-screen device. This in part may be why advertisers are more reluctant to spend their money on ads in a virtual newspaper. This poses a problem. Critics and marketing experts are saying the reason for this is because the focus of the newspaper staff is remaining on print – but it is not the staff that is at fault. The *clients* don't want to advertise on little hand-held devices like mobile phones because it seems their message is more fleeting in this form and stands more of a chance at being lost or ignored.

A physical newspaper is enjoyed in its entirety, rather than in bits and pieces. People are more inclined to read more of the paper when it appears in physical form. You open it up and scan everything on a page. It is accessible all at once. Ads do not get ignored as easily. There is also something relaxing about a physical paper. It puts the reader in a more relaxed mood. Those who buy and use devices for their news are generally not as relaxed. Things are more fast-paced, you jump around more because the screen is so small – which in turn creates a shorter attention span. People with short attention spans are usually not *relaxed*. This is not good for advertisers. The big challenge for creating revenue in the future rests on convincing advertisers to go digital. The future seems geared more to tablets than with smaller devices, so this will help with the presentation of newspapers.

Advertising is something books are not involved with, so physical books will remain stronger for much longer. Newspapers will still remain in physical form, but seem to lack a strong future with printed versions. Printed versions are no longer an exclusive, viable medium to drive their companies financially. This means they must take and use every outlet available to the best of their ability.

Following is a list of options newspapers must consider in order to survive – which book publishers should take special note of in case they are one day confronted with a similar situation. Should books ever get to that position, many of these options may no longer apply, due mainly to the fast-paced changes we continue to experience with information-based technologies. Some of these points apply right now to the world of books and should be employed while other options, like advertising, may not apply at all. Newspapers, however, should take careful note of all ten.

TOP TEN THINGS NEWSPAPERS MUST DO TO SURVIVE

1. Subscriptions

With all things considered, the best option newspapers have is to offer digital subscriptions – but it must be done in a way to attract subscribers. People have always subscribed to physical newspapers, but often shy away from paying for the same thing online. News is found in many places online for free. Extra value and/or information needs to be incorporated into online subscriptions, much like public TV and cable

TV does, in order to get subscriptions going. Creative options should be employed, often using locally-based or niche-based advantages that cannot be found elsewhere. This is the answer for papers having a tough time with subscriptions. Some are thriving in this area, like *The Wall Street Journal* and *Financial Times* (niche-based and needed). The strong reputation of *The New York Times* has enabled it to achieve, as of this writing, just under 500,000 digital subscriptions. This would be great for most papers, but still puts the *Times* in a challenging position and they are working to do better. Many small market papers will never achieve enough digital subscriptions to make it, so cutting costs as much as possible and employing the tips below, will be the best options to take.

2. Community

Some papers are trying to figure out successful business plans that involve social media on a community level. Bringing community together for various reasons rather than just sharing news, could play a big part in the future of newspapers. This creates loyalty and, if done in certain niches, can create strong loyalties. The *Boston Globe*, *Washington Post* and others have begun to use a strong, open source Facebook-based program called NewsCloud in this capacity, which also involves direct input from readers. This leads into our next area.

3. Online Interaction

Newspaper sites have not allowed as many comments from readers on their stories, although other sites that do allow them end up with more page views. The two major hang-ups, it seems, that keeps online newspapers from blossoming, are that 1) professional journalists do not like to share the territory with opinionated non-professionals and interact with the public on an even level. After all, brain surgeons do not invite people off the street to come in and do surgery, so why should journalists do the equivalent? The answer is that journalism is not brain surgery. If people get things wrong, true journalists can correct them. Healthy debate can occur when people are invited in. You won't have Frankenstein's brain put into your grandmother like with brain surgery, so journalists should loosen up and relax a little. This leads us to number 2) journalists do not want to spend time interacting with user groups online as much as they want to do real journalism, which is their true job and what they signed up for. Unfortunately, the profession is changing and, like in many fields, online interaction is becoming a necessity. If the public is engaged and helps journalists do their jobs, it will keep the journalists working and maintaining their jobs. Like it or not, news is now a dialogue.

Sometimes, however, the interaction that takes place is a one-way "theft," and large news organizations are tired of people taking their stories and posting them as their own. This also happens with the piracy of books. News stories are shorter, however, and take only hours to write rather than years. Some believe it should be okay for links to be shared, rather than copying the stories, because it gives proper credit, brings readers to the actual news source and can create loyal customers as a result. Some still do not agree with this. For example, iCopyright has an infringement detection system that the Associated Press has been using in an effort to protect their material from what is being called the "link economy." The AP is receiving its share of criticism for employing this. It seems the book industry might benefit even more from iCopyright, depending on cost and effectiveness.

4. Mobile Apps

Smartphones are becoming popular as a way to access news, so news organizations are developing things like iphone applications. Now, for the first time, people are starting to pay for news through these mobile apps, making this a good direction to go.

5. Revamping the Corporate Structure

Newspapers have a certain structure that has become incompatible with the fast pace of the Internet and the creative impulses that drive it. Creativity and new ideas need to be nourished so that corporate structures can move in new directions faster. For example, the engineers at Google get to work on side projects that attract them through the company's "20 percent time" rule. All kinds of new Google products have sprung up as a result.

6. Twitter

Most would agree that Twitter has become the best and fastest way to report breaking news. Real time updates work great and can bring people to newspaper websites to view live streaming video of breaking events. The more creative a news organization is, the more Twitter can be employed.

7. Sifting and Purifying

Little time is spent in the U. S. on visiting newspaper websites, so papers must devise ways to become robust clearinghouses for information. Since linking technology is the wave of the future and many spread links to online newspaper stories, with or without permission, journalists need to do the same with other sites and stories. The challenge will be in the verification of truthfulness and accuracy – but journalists should be better at this than others, due to their training, expertise and networking skills. Help those who help you. In addition, bits and pieces relating to certain stories can be gathered from numerous sources to strengthen the value of news stories, something that journalists should be doing at every online paper with the right search tools.

8. Analyze and Contextualize

Adding commentaries to news stories can also be useful, whether it be from blogs, tweets or personal journalistic opinion. Time sensitive stories are no longer in the domain of newspapers, so adding context to stories is becoming more important. This approach will make each story unique to the reporting agency and if done well, success will follow. If newspaper sites fail to do this, others will do it and they will be left behind. The fact is, everyone is on the same equal footing as journalists so it's time for the professionals to step up and use their expertise as journalists to outshine the amateurs. Proving it over time will win the audience in their favor.

9. Higher Quality Niche News

The trends point to a future with specialization. Doing stories in a unique way takes time, and therefore covering the entire gamut of subject areas will be more difficult. Developing a niche and creating a strong audience will insure the success of the more serious and competitive news organizations. Trying to please everyone just isn't going to work anymore unless you have a huge staff and are capable of paying them to do massive, in-depth stories that will be needed for the organization to succeed. This means that successful newspapers will be morphing into magazines to a certain degree, being forced to adopt their style of reporting.

10. Employ Multiple Platforms

With news, the shift from print into electronic formats has happened. Whether newspapers continue to flourish in electronic formats is yet to be determined. Other less proficient but determined people are spreading the news around – like bloggers and news-related sites that do not necessarily have official connections to physical newspapers.

Newspaper companies have no choice but to employ multiple platforms in order to stay afloat. In general, most revenue still comes from physical newspapers, which advertisers prefer. Electronic customers don't believe in parting with their dollars to get Internet based news. It doesn't seem to matter if a legitimate newspaper is involved or not. So news companies must get creative and make it worthwhile for customers to pay. Advertising in electronic formats must be the focus now or very soon, but should be done creatively in order for it to work.

News must also be presented to fit with mobile devices, social networks and websites as much as it has been perfected for physical papers throughout the years. People are too dependent on technology to approach things any differently. So the last and most important thing to say about newspapers is to the consumer. Newspapers in general can no longer survive in print form only, so make the switch. Please subscribe to the digital form of your newspaper even if you prefer the paper version. Otherwise, you may not be able to get any news at all from them in the future. It is better to get your news from trusted, professional and experienced sources – and this includes local news that might be harder to find online, from outside sources. Support you local paper. If you prefer a physical one that you can share and give to others, please subscribe. More importantly, keep your local paper alive in whatever form that it needs to exist.

The Bottom Line

Newspapers must contend with all these things because news is short, choppy and fast like the Internet, which suits it perfectly. News becomes old and is no longer "news" after a day or two, but books are timeless. You can kick back with a book and relax. It's the same with the creation of content. To write a book usually requires no rushing. People take years to write books, but news stories must happen now – quickly, before anyone else can break the story or before the news gets too old. Newspapers jump around from one story to the next, while books often stick to one main subject.

The point is that books, for now, are safer than newspapers as physical objects. They will not disappear down an uncertain black hole in cyberspace like newspapers are starting to do. Many people will always prefer a physical newspaper, but there may come a day when they will be almost non-existent – which is sad. Physical books are not as time sensitive. Therefore, they do not lose their importance or need to be discarded as quickly. They can be treasured. News can also be treasured – but only briefly. We wish newspapers the best of luck and good health in their transformation.

Chapter Seven

Summary

This book is not an effort to turn back the hands of time and eliminate e-book technology. That would be an impossible task. The entire technology as a whole is part of the path of human evolution and ingenuity. The paper book purist must learn to live with this reality – but also to inject some common sense into the mayhem of technology, when appropriate.

Standard books will still be preferred by large numbers of people for many years to come, and this book is a rallying cry for the purists. Although Neanderthals were an evolutionary dead-end, it is yet to be determined if e-books or paper books will follow the same path. It could happen either way. But in all likliehood, both will remain and coexist with each other for many years to come.

E-books are still being perfected. They are new and in their infancy. But the advent of e-books is *not* as revolutionary as the introduction of the printing press. The introduction of e-books has instead been likened (by experts) to the point in history when mankind began replacing clay tablet libraries with text written on scrolls. This shift demanded an entirely new way of storing and processing information. It is a matter of preference. Clay tablets took up more room, similar to paper books today. Each page was a separate tablet, so you could not easily carry around even one book! You had to use the library. Paper scrolls made this more bearable.

Today, that one clay tablet "page" would be equal in size to a normal paper book – or a digital reader. It's just a matter of preference as to whether you'd like to carry around one book with you at a time, or hundreds. Many will agree that we've gotten to the point of overkill. Do we really need to have hundreds, or even thousands, of books at our fingertips? Some people do. But most do not. Some are just intrigued, or even intoxicated, by the idea that their entire library is in their purse or pocket. This is ideal for avid readers who constantly travel, or are homeless with no living space. Everyone else in between will be using their own personal preference in making their choices.

Many people have a digital reader and still buy paper books. Their own personal situations dictate which format they will use. This usage is balanced, but there are also extremes. Those who have completely enmeshed themselves in the digital revolution show cold indifference to paper books, and some even hold them in contempt. *How dare these relics of the past remain loved and cherished by the masses! The electronic age has arrived!*

This cold attitude is juxtaposed with the emotional connection many have with their physical books, magazines and newspapers. These people are shocked at the idea of everyday physical objects disappearing from normal view. Physical newspapers are becoming less common. I have seen more than one person driven to tears at the idea of losing their physical newspaper. Not to mention the thousands who have lost their jobs, and the many more who may be forced to follow.

The newer jobs today are going to young, savvy people riding the electronic wave, while the old guard – unable to mount this wave or grasp the needed trends or skills – sit on the sidelines and wonder how to feed their families. This is not a complaint. It is the reality. If you want to work and feed your family it is almost a requirement to join the digital revolution in some way, shape or form – which makes everyone in society more dependent on electronic and digital components.

Technology Overkill

Technology in itself is not such a bad thing. It is the overkill that is bad – all of the superficial junk and apps, cluttering up these devices. One could argue that *paper* takes up more room than these applications and devices. That is true. But you must consider the time wasted and distractions created from these applications and devices. Paper instructions – like with an owner's manual for example – do not require codes to operate and don't crash or freeze. With computers, everything must be done perfectly regarding code or certain steps of instruction – otherwise you cannot accomplish any of your intended tasks. There are no gray areas with computers like in real life, which can allow you to explore multiple possibilities for reachable answers. With computer programs, one strict requirement leads to another and before you know it, you are caught in a cyber-world that offers no escape if you want to get anything done. The time invested can be enormous if just one glitch pops up that requires you to troubleshoot it. Often times the bug is buried under layers of incomprehensible code that only an expert can reach. We've all been there, and these continuous loops can be extremely frustrating. Many of us have smashed an electronic device, which can be a liberating experience. You vs. computerized device; device is winning; it refuses to cooperate despite your best efforts; you smash device; you win. This theory is testable and has a high rate of success. If one stops and thinks about an easier alternative like using a typewriter (which would allow the work to get done), it can lead to a yearning for simpler days.

Social Dysfunction

Relying on computerized devices for virtually everything in today's world really does take some of the warmth and meaning away from us. Things are colder; more distant. We have further separated ourselves from each other because social skills are not needed as much. For example, we are texting people than calling them or exchanging ideas with them in person. Verbal inflection on the phone or body language in person, or even a touch, can be used far better to convey our ideas.

We are sending books, documents or "hellos" electronically, rather than acting face-to-face, warmly, as a friend. The distance has continued to increase slowly, over time, and with each new invention.

Examples of technology robbing us of social and personal growth go on and on, to the point where we, as a whole, are beginning to act colder and more distant to each other, and are becoming more self-centered. The younger generations experience extreme bullying in the physical sense and on the Internet, and we never had such severe problems with previous generations. This degree of bullying among young people has become epidemic and is caused by the *distance* that we have created between each other with our more "convenient" technology. All areas of society are being affected, but young people cannot handle it as well as others, so it often appears in more drastic forms with them. Across the board, with all ages, the price we are paying for personal technology is becoming dysfunctional – with individuals within society, and with society as a whole.

It may be argued that personal technology is actually bringing us closer together. This is true, if you are referring to the sharing of information. It is done faster and with more data. But it is done from afar, with the exclusion of personal contact and the ability to share the information personally and closely, with clear emotional contact and expression, as we have done from the moment we became humans – thousands upon thousands of years ago. And now, a number of versatile little gadgets are proceeding to yank this form of humanity away, with all of its warmth and meaning, completely out of our lives and we *go along with it*. We accept it blindly, without even batting an eye.

Marching to the Tune of E-books

This is not to say that e-books or their reading devices are the cause for society's ills. They are only a small part of this new wave of technology – but they are, nevertheless, a good representation of what is happening to our culture.

Traditional paper books do not force you into buying a "personal device" just so you can read. Some do not like the coldness of these gadgets and choose to avoid them. E-books play only a small role in that scenario – but enough so that some people clearly *do not like them*. The bottom line is that paper books are not going anywhere. Despite the big push to eliminate them, it is not going to happen. When music formats changed, there were 8-track tapes, followed by cassettes and during this entire time vinyl records were still used. Cassettes were relegated to people's vehicles, while the high quality sound from vinyl stayed at home in the high-end stereo systems of the day. This is similar to what we have today with e-books. Most people tend to be homebodies. People out and about, who are on the go, will choose e-books while those wishing to remain comfortable at home opt for a normal paper one. That seems to be the general consensus today.

Paper books, however, will not disappear like vinyl records did. When CDs came along, vinyl records almost completely vanished – despite the higher quality sound they still produce to this day. In the bigger scheme of things, vinyl records were not around for very long, but books have been around for centuries. Paper books will not vanish in the same way as vinyl because music and books are two different things. For a consumer, music comes from out of the air and cannot be seen, while books require a more direct and tactile experience. People are less inclined to give up a more physical connection to something and thereby distance themselves from the experience.

When e-books first came along, they were rejected by consumers for *years*, and did not take hold until after relentless marketing efforts and continued improvements in the technology. Today, these efforts appeal more to a younger "techie" crowd that has little experience with the value of a real book. As a result, you can now "highlight" in certain e-books and even "write in the margins," because people are trying to mimic the intimate aspects of having a real book. But somehow, for those who know the difference, it just isn't the same. E-books will always remain cold and distant by comparison.

The Push-Button Society

The goal of e-reader companies is to mimic a real book so well that the consumer stops making the comparison altogether and accepts an e-reader with the same comfort as a normal book. The choice is yours. Will you accept the counterfeit or stay with the original format? People in general are lazy and that is a big reason why e-books have begun to flourish. For example, they would rather push a button than physically turn a page. Our society wants to provide us with everything just by the push of a button. That seems to be the goal – but it takes away direct experience and a certain type of richness from life in many cases. Any invention that allows you to push a button instead of actually doing something will make you, as an inventor, rich. Patent something even remotely useful that contains this feature and watch the money roll in. It doesn't matter what it is. People are so lazy they will buy it immediately. A nation of obese people cannot be bothered with extending any more energy than necessary, when they can just lift a finger and press. Otherwise, it's just too much trouble. And that includes turning the physical page of a book! It's very sad.

This laziness is the biggest threat to paper books – along with policy makers. The best thing we can do to avoid cutbacks of paper books is to reverse some of the political decisions they have made, educate them on how to repair the "dumbing down" of society and keep them away from high tech lobbyists, sweet deals and "pay-offs" under the table.

There are more reasons why e-books appeal to people, other than supporting their laziness. Certain e-books can be cheaper than a normal book and they take up less space. But laziness still plays a role in how people acquire their books. Unless you are in a store, you must wait for a paper book to be shipped to you. People are too lazy to go into a store and experience additional discoveries, meet others or enrich their lives in a multitude of other ways while there. They would rather just press a button and download a "book," rather than visit a store or wait a few days for a physical version to come in the mail. If time is a concern, like having to write a book report, this is understandable. But that is usually not the case.

Patience is a virtue and older people tend to have more than younger ones. But everyone, old or young, has been conditioned to desire instant gratification in recent years and are of the belief that they should not have to wait for anything. Pushing buttons is the most desired solution. It saves time. A few hundred years ago kings had everything done for them at the snap of a finger by having numerous servants fill their various needs. Today we all strive to be kings, running our little "kingdoms" from computer terminals, and the younger you are, the more inclined you are to believe that you are, in fact, a king and deserve to have everything that you could possibly desire served up to you instantly and for free (if possible) on a silver platter. All with the press of a button. That is the goal. We must stop conditioning our youth in this way.

The idea of working hard for anything is becoming ancient history. The goal is shortcuts. Creating a shortcut to success without working for it is the goal of virtually everyone today, especially the young. In years past, people were more inclined to roll up their sleeves and work hard for their success. Today, however, many young people try to avoid it like the plague. *This is not the fault of young people.* The world is full of great kids. It is the fault of the technology that has been pushed upon them. The technology is creating self-serving monsters that have a warped sense of values based on the instant gratification that the technology promises – and in many cases provides.

You cannot and should not put a stop to progress. Progress is good. But the way we *use it* needs to be carefully examined. Whenever any new innovation or piece of technology comes along, it is best to ask yourself one thing in a deep and careful way. You should ask, "How will this device affect me, as a person?"

Instead of asking what it will do *for* you, you must ask what will it do *to you*, as a person. After considering this carefully, from every angle, only then should you make your decision about purchasing one or not. Be awake. Be aware of who you are, what you are really doing with your choices, and how they will or will not improve you – truly improve you – as a moral, ethical, caring, conscious person.

Experiencing e-books and e-readers gives you a different view of the world and a different way of interacting with it. They are certainly not evil devices and this is not a black or white issue. Many people read with e-books *and* paper ones. E-books and e-readers can be good in some cases and I would wholeheartedly recommend them for certain situations. There is room for both versions of books in this world – e-books and paper. This book, however, is a reminder to you of the value of a traditional book. E-books, after all, are imitating the real thing and the bottom line is that no matter what you do, there is nothing like the *real thing*. You can imitate it, but you will never replace it – not unless the improvements become so vast and overwhelming that they completely override the format of original books. Based on the studies and preferences presented in this book, this scenario will never happen.

Some improvements over standard books are evident, depending on the consumer, but the intrinsic design of a paper book has too many irreplaceable features. Therefore, e-books and paper books must live together and share the market. The evolution of the book market is fully up to you, the consumer. It is believed there will always be enough people who love standard books so much that they will always be around. It is also hoped that those who enjoy e-books will still value printed versions to some degree, for the various reasons put forth in this work – enough so that in many years we might still be able to say, after centuries of success, "Long live printed books."

www.ingramcontent.com/pod-product-compliance
Lightning Source LLC
Chambersburg PA
CBHW071254050326
40690CB00011B/2400